WITNESS
AT SAND CREEK

WITNESS
AT SAND CREEK

The Life and Letters of Silas Soule

Nancy Niero

Exact Rush Multimedia Publishing
Exact Rush, LLC.
353 W. Greensboro Ct.
Boise, ID 83706

Exact Rush Multimedia Publishing and the Exact Rush logo are trademarks of Exact Rush, LLC.

Copyright © Nancy Niero, 2025

Cover Design: Exact Rush, LLC.
Cover Image © Denver Public Library Special Collections, 22202
Inset Image © Nancy Niero, 2024

All rights reserved. No part of this publication may be reproduced or transmitted in any form or by any means, electronic or mechanical, including photocopying, recording, or any information storage or retrieval system, without prior permission in writing from the publishers.

Exact Rush, LLC. does not have control over, or responsibility for, any third-party websites referred to or in this book. All internet addresses given in this book were correct at the time of going to press. The author and publisher regret any inconvenience caused if addresses have changed or sites have ceased to exist, but can accept no responsibility for any such changes.

Library of Congress Control Number: 2025913002

ISBN: 979-8-9898235-5-0

Author Land Acknowledgement

This book was written in Denver, Colorado, on land that was traveled by the Cheyenne, Ute, and Arapaho Indigenous people for centuries. I acknowledge this land, this place, is the ancestral home where the people hunted and traveled. It is important for me to acknowledge the land as a white woman of European descent, elder, Christian pastor, and descendant of Ellis Island immigrants to honor the original inhabitants. As an activist, I pledge myself to the work of disrupting systems of oppression that led to the dispossession of Indigenous people from the land and that have continued to deny their rights to self-determination.

The Cheyenne Ute, and Arapaho people are not a people of the past. They are a people of the present.

Editorial Note

Every reasonable effort has been made to honor the textual integrity of these nineteenth-century letters while preparing them for publication. Because they have circulated through multiple hands and formats, private family archives, typed carbon copies, microfilm, and now digital scans housed at the Library of Congress, the Kansas State Historical Society, the University of Denver, the Denver Public Library, and History Colorado, no single witness can claim absolute primacy. Over 150 years, archivists and editors have introduced minor variants in spelling, punctuation, and even phrasing. Inevitably, slight discrepancies may remain; they reflect both the complex provenance of the materials and the interpretive judgments required of any modern transcription.

I invite future cultural historians and those curious to expand the worldview of Silas Soule to explore these letters with this caveat.

A portion of book proceeds will go to the Sand Creek Massacre Foundation. To learn more about the foundation, or to donate, visit sandcreekmassacrefoundation.org

Site of the Sand Creek Massacre.
©Nancy Niero, 2024

Praise for *Witness at Sand Creek*

"Words have power, and the historical words of Silas Soule reveal the life of a man who showed up and worked for justice by speaking truth. Nancy Niero adeptly analyzes and interprets Soule's words from letters he wrote to not only show Soule as a witness to history around the Sand Creek Massacre, but also as a man who put his faith into action to speak out against it. Niero's words also encourage readers to create a life of witness by acknowledging the past and working to make the future better. She calls us all to be more like Soule, especially today when the world needs more truth-telling to make justice happen."
– Lisa Barnett, Ph.D., Associate Professor of American Religious History at Phillips Theological Seminary (Tulsa, OK)

"Silas Soule's story of courage in the service of confronting overwhelming injustice is a lesson for all of us. In these pages, Silas tells us the story in his own words with an expert helping hand. This book will be essential for anyone looking to learn more about the true history of the American West."
– Sam Bock, Director of Interpretation and Publications, Managing Editor of *The Colorado Magazine*, **and lead exhibition developer for** *The Sand Creek Massacre: The Betrayal that Changed Cheyenne and Arapaho People Forever*

"The story of Silas Soule and his pivotal role in resisting the murderous rampage of John Chivington's soldiers at the Sand Creek Massacre is a history that has been told primarily through his letters of testimony documenting the genocidal horrors he witnessed and his resistance to the violence. Nancy Niero brings Soule's letters into a new light by inviting the reader along on her racial justice pilgrimage to see the massacre with new eyes and a deeper understanding. With each letter from Soule, she provides context and commentary that prompts the reader to see the larger history of this horrific massacre literally from the ground up. Niero's descriptions of landscape and terrain intersect with interviews, observations, and analysis that provide a unique window into the story of peaceful Arapaho and Cheyenne who were brutally murdered by Chivington's soldiers. Reading the history through Nancy's eyes was an important opportunity for me to expand my learning and reflection on the Sand Creek Massacre."
– Loring Abeyta, Ph.D., John Wesley Iliff Senior Adjunct of Religion and Society

"This is a book of journeys – physical and spiritual, internal and external, ethical and moral, historical and contemporary. Dr. Neiro intertwines the experiences and heart of Silas Soule, expressed through a series of his letters, with her own transformative exploration of social justice as she retraces the footprints of Silas's life from 1860 to 1865. The eternal legacy of his morality in standing up against the unconscionable Sand Creek Massacre serves as a basis for the author's call to seek our own paths towards healing, social justice, and a future without the inhumanity to which Silas Soule was a witness."
– Alexa Roberts, Board Member, Sand Creek Massacre Foundation

Table of Contents

Timeline	XI
Foreword by Eric J. Carpio	XIX
Prologue: Finding Meaning in a 30 Year Journey of Love and Loss	1
1. The Life of Silas Soule	9
2. The Letters, 1860 – Leaving Kansas	27
3. The Letter, 1861 – A Mining Life	39
4. The Letters, 1862 – War, Hope, and Family	47
5. The Letters, 1863 – Denver	65
6. The Letters, Winter-Spring 1864 – From Fort Garland to Fort Lyon, Their World is About to Mightily Change	73
7. The Letters, Summer-Fall 1864 – Witnessing Peace, Witnessing Death	101
8. The Last Letter, 1865 – Repair Work	147
9. Racial Justice Pilgrimages with Silas	153
Epilogue: Meaning Making in the 21st Century	175
Afterword by Gary L. Roberts	181
Acknowledgements	197
Bibliography	201

Timeline

July 26, 1838 — Born in Bath, ME to Amasa and Sophia Soule.

1852 — Sophia read *Uncle Tom's Cabin*, by Harriet Beecher Stowe, out loud to her family, which inspired abolitionist Amasa and family to join the New England Emigrant Company, created by New England abolitionists to keep Kansas free from enslavement.[1]

Oct. 1855 — Silas arrived in Lawrence, Kansas Territory, with his two sisters, Annie and Emily with their mother, Sophia, and joined his father and brother, William Lloyd Garrison, who arrived in Lawrence in November 1854. They all settled in Coal Creek in a log cabin. They, along with other Congregationalists, started Plymouth Congregational Church, a sanctuary originally made of hay bales.

---

1. A.B. MacDonald, "She Looks Back Seventy-Five Years to the Founding of Lawrence," *Kansas City Star*, January 13, 1929, 1.

1859

July 1859	Silas joined nine other men from Lawrence to break Dr. John Doy, the general conductor of the Underground Railroad in Kansas Territory, out of jail in St. Joseph, MO, after he was arrested conducting 13 formerly enslaved people to freedom. They are known as "The Immortal Ten." The capture and rescue was news throughout the country and brought wide support to the movement in Kansas. A photo of "The Immortal Ten" hangs in the Kansas State Historical Museum in Topeka, KS. Those Immortal 10 abolitionists are Doy's son Charles, George R. Hay, Joseph Gardner, Joshua A. Pike, Jacob Senix, Thomas Simmons, Silas, John E. Stewart, James B. Abbott, and S.J. Willis.
Oct. 16-18, 1859	Abolitionist John Brown led a raid with a group of supporters on the federal armory and arsenal at Harpers Ferry, WV. Brown was captured. Ten of his men were killed, including his son, Oliver.
Dec. 2, 1859	Brown was executed on December 2, 1859.

1860

Feb. 17, 1860	A group of Kansans, recruited by Kansas abolitionist Richard J. Hinton, including Silas, arrived in Harrisburg, PA, to break out two of John Brown's accomplices, Albert Hazlett and Aaron Stevens from jail in Charlestown, WV. They scatter to do reconnaissance

work and Silas is sent to explore Virginia. While not named, Silas may have actually gotten into the jail as a "jovial, half-drunken Irishman," and spoke with the prisoners, who resisted the jail break.[2] By February 25, the disappointing decision was made to abandon the attempts to break out Hazlett and Stevens due to heavy snows.[3] They were executed on March 16, 1860.

Feb. 21, 1860	Silas wrote to old friend George Cutter, from Harrisburg, PA.
March 1860	Met poet Walt Whitman, William Wilde Thayer, Charles W. Eldridge, in Boston, MA.
May 9, 1860	Wrote a letter to Thayer, Eldridge, and Richard J. Hinton from Coal Creek, Kansas Territory. Silas is about to leave for Pikes Peak and the gold fields of the Colorado Territory (C.T.) to join his brother and cousin.
Sept. 26, 1860	Amasa Soule, Silas' father, died in Lawrence, Kansas Territory.

1861

Jan. 29, 1861	Kansas was admitted to the Union as the 34th state.
April 12, 1861	Fort Sumter was attacked by the Confederate Army which starts the American Civil War.

---

2. Thomas Wentworth Higginson, *Cheerful Yesterdays*, The American Negro, His History and Literature, (New York, NY: Arno Press), 1968, 233.
3. Richard J. Hinton, *John Brown and His Men*, The American Negro, His History and Literature, (New York, NY: Arno Press, 1968), 524-525.

July 21, 1861	Wrote to old friend Major James B. Abbott from Missourie City, C.T.
Dec. 11, 1861	Silas enlisted in Blackhawk, C.T. and is appointed 1st Lieutenant.

1862

Jan. 8, 1862	Wrote to poet Walt Whitman from somewhere in Gilpin County.
Feb. 20-21, 1862	**Battle of Valverde, near Val Verde, NM**
March 12, 1862	Wrote to Walt Whitman from Fort Union, NM
March 26-8, 1862	**Battle of Glorietta Pass, near Pecos, NM**
April 14-15, 1862	**Battle of Peralto, Peralto, NM**
May or June 1862	Wrote to Walt Whitman from Camp Valverde at Fort Craig, NM.

1863

Aug. 21, 1863	**Quantrill's Raid, also known as the Lawrence Raid, Lawrence, KS.**
Sept. 4, 1863	Wrote to sister, Emily, from Denver, C.T
Oct. 11, 1863	Wrote to sister, Annie, from Central City, C.T.

1864

Jan. 3, 1864	Wrote to Col. John Chivington

	from Fort Garland, C.T.
Feb. 18, 1864	Wrote to Col. John Chivington from Guadalupe Conejos, C.T.
Feb. 22, 1864	Wrote to mother, Sophia from Guadelupe Conejos, C.T.
April 7, 1864	Wrote to unknown recipient from Fort Garland, C.T.
April 14, 1864	Promoted to rank of Captain, Co. D. 1 Colorado Cavalry, per military records. Assigned to recruiting services.
May 19, 1864	**Cherry Creek floods in Denver.**
June 2, 1864	Wrote to his mother from Camp Fillmore, C.T.
June 17, 1864	Wrote to Annie from Fort Lyon, C.T.
July 16, 1864	Wrote to Annie from Fort Lyon, C.T.
July 29, 1864	Wrote to his mother from Fort Lyon, C.T.
Aug. 15, 1864	Wrote to Annie from Fort Lyon, C.T.
Sept. 10, 1864	Silas went to the Smoky Hill Council with Major Wynkoop, Lt. Hardin. Lt. Cramer, Lt. Phillips, with Black Kettle, Cheyenne chief, and Left Hand, Arapaho chief, and other chiefs from both Cheyenne and Arapaho.[4]

---

4. Report of the Secretary of War, February 14, 1867, Washington City, Major Edward W. Wynkoop Testimony on March 20, 1865, 84, 85.

Sept. 28, 1864	Silas attended Camp Weld Council, Denver, C.T.
Oct. 11, 1864	Wrote a letter to Col. John Chivington from Fort Lyon, C.T.
Oct. 16, 1864	Wrote to Major Edward W. Wynkoop from Fort Garland, C.T.
Oct. 17, 1864	Wrote to Col. John Chivington from Fort Lyon, C.T.
Oct. 30, 1864	Wrote to Annie from Fort Lyon, C.T.
Nov. 25, 1864	Wrote to Major Scott J. Anthony from Fort Lyon, C.T.
Nov. 29, 1864	**Sand Creek Massacre, where 230 Cheyenne and Arapaho elders, women and children, living in a peaceful camp were horrifically murdered by Colorado soldiers under the command of Col. John Chivington, a Methodist minister.**
Dec. 14, 1864	Wrote to Major Edward Wynkoop from Fort Lyon, C.T.
Dec. 18, 1864	Wrote to his mother from Fort Lyon, C.T.

1865

Jan. 8, 1865	Wrote to his mother from Fort Lyon, C.T.
Jan. 30, 1865	According to the Company Muster-In and Descriptive Roll in his military records, Silas was 26 years old, his occupation was soldier, his eye color

	is grey, hair is sandy, his complexion is fair, his height is 5'6", his enlistment period was three years; he mustered in on April 15, 1864 in Fort Garland, C.T.[5]
Jan. 31, 1865	Mustered out of service, per military records. Appointed Adjunct Provost Marshall in Denver.
Feb. 9, 1865	**Congressional Inquiry into the Sand Creek Massacre begins in Denver, C.T.**
Feb. 16, 1865	Silas was the first witness at the Congressional Inquiry.
April 1, 1865	Silas married Hersa Coberly in Denver, C.T.
April 9, 1865	**Confederate General Robert E. Lee signs surrender documents at Appomattox, Virginia and the American Civil War ends.**
April 15, 1865	**President Abraham Lincoln was assassinated.**
April 20, 1865	Silas wrote in a communique that he denies the accusation by John Chivington that he stole buffalo robes in the aftermath of the Sand Creek Massacre.
April 23, 1865	Silas was assassinated near 15th and Arapaho Streets in Denver, C.T.

---

5. National Archives, Military Records, Silas Stillman Soule.

Foreword

I first met Nancy Niero through a phone call. It was brief, thoughtful, and direct — qualities I would come to associate with her work ever since. She reached out to say that she was retracing the journey of Silas Soule by following a collection of letters he had written before and after the Sand Creek Massacre. What I didn't know until my conversation with Nancy, was that Silas had traveled through Colorado's San Luis Valley in the early months of 1864 — mere months before the horrific events of November 29, 1864.

Several of Silas's letters were written from Fort Garland, a United States military post built in 1858 — ten years after the signing of the Treaty of Guadalupe. The treaty, which ended the Mexican-American War, converted five hundred and twenty-five thousand square miles from the hands of Mexico to the United States, including a portion of Colorado known as the San Luis Valley. Fort Garland emerged in the valley to facilitate American, primarily Anglo, expansion into this new American territory.

Today, Fort Garland is a community museum of History Colorado, the state's historical society, where I serve as the director. Nancy contacted me to learn about Fort Garland and the various places and experiences Silas referenced in his letters.

But Nancy wasn't just doing archival research, she wanted to walk where he walked and see what he had seen. She was on a pilgrimage.

That word — pilgrimage — is important. It speaks to a deeper kind of engagement, one that transcends historical interest. Nancy wasn't merely following a trail of letters. She was engaging with a legacy. She was listening.

And that's what this book does. It listens carefully to the voice of a man who, in one of the darkest hours of American history, chose to stand on the side of truth, integrity, and humanity — at tremendous personal cost. In these pages, Nancy brings Silas Soule's letters to life, not as dusty artifacts, but as dispatches from the frontlines of moral decision-making. In doing so, she invites us to consider an urgent question: What compels a regular person to stand on the right side of history in the face of severe consequence?

The Man Behind the Letters

Silas Soule was born in Maine in 1838, into a family of abolitionists who later moved to Kansas to support the Free State cause. In Kansas, Silas cut his teeth on political struggle and violence. He worked alongside figures like John Brown, wrote letters to Walt Whitman, and became involved in the Underground Railroad. He saw the brutality of systems built on oppression — and also the fragility of the human conscience when placed under pressure. He saw how easily right and wrong could be confused when filtered through the lens of power, ambition, or fear.

That early crucible of violence and idealism shaped Silas into a man of profound principle. But it wasn't until years later that his moral principles would be tested to the limit.

In November 1864, Silas was stationed at Fort Lyon in Colorado Territory under Colonel John Chivington. It was there that he witnessed — and refused to participate in — the Sand Creek Massacre, an unprovoked attack on a peaceful village of Cheyenne and Arapaho people in eastern Colorado. Silas disobeyed orders. He kept his men from engaging in the slaughter. He wrote detailed letters testifying to what he saw. And, then he told the truth to a U.S. military commission, implicating Chivington and others in the atrocities.

Five months later, Silas was shot dead in the streets of Denver. He was 26 years old.

Fort Garland

Reading Silas's letters through the lens of our collective work at the Fort Garland Museum & Cultural Center, I'm reminded that history is not fixed — it is shaped, preserved, and often sanitized.

For nearly seventy years, the interpretation at the Fort Garland Museum showcased a single narrative about the American West, one centered on Kit Carson as the heroic frontiersman. Carson was sent to command Fort Garland after his brutal campaign against the Navajo to "deal with the Ute problem." Eventually, the Ute Treaty of 1868, also known as the 'Kit Carson Treaty,' was signed. The treaty resulted in the removal of all Ute people from their traditional homelands in the San Luis Valley.

The museum's interpretation reflected a particular mythology, one deeply embedded in American memory — an image of manifest destiny, conquest, and "civilizing" the frontier. It was also, undeniably, a story built on silence and erasure.

In 2018, we made a decision that had been long overdue, we deinstalled a Kit Carson exhibition that had been in place for sixty-eight years. In its place, in 2021, we opened a new exhibition in collaboration with renowned artist Chip Thomas, *Unsilenced: Indigenous Enslavement in Southern Colorado*. The change was not cosmetic — it was foundational. *Unsilenced* marked a shift toward truth-telling, and toward centering stories that had been excluded or suppressed. This kind of work is slow and often difficult, but it's also essential.

The truth-telling that Nancy is pursuing in this book is the same truth-telling we aspire to at the museum. It is about reclaiming complexity and leaning into difficult conversations. It's about holding space for multiple voices, especially those that history has attempted to erase. It is about reminding ourselves, and our communities, that honesty is the foundation of justice and acknowledgement is the first step toward healing.

In one of my first conversations with Nancy, I couldn't help but to think about the connections between Silas and another former commander at Fort Garland, Colonel Samuel Forster Tappan. In the research that emerged from *Unsilenced*, we learned that while stationed at Fort Garland, Tappan had attempted to curb slave raids and even sent requests to his counterparts in New Mexico Territory to intervene. The assistance never materialized.

I often hear people defend Kit Carson's violence against Native people by saying he was "a man of his time" or that "he was just following orders." But Nancy's book reminds us that history includes people like Silas and Tappan, who were also men of their time and yet chose differently. Both Silas and Tappan were soldiers. They were white. Both lived in a violent, racist, and expansionist society. Yet, both chose to speak out against the oppression of Native people. Silas and Tappan are examples of people who stood at a moral crossroads and made the more difficult choice. Their courage reveals that there was always another way.

On an interesting note, Colonel Tappan would be appointed to head a military commission to investigate John Chivington for his role in the Sand Creek Massacre.

The Letters

When we talk about moral courage, we often frame it in grand, cinematic terms. But reading Silas Soule's letters, as Nancy presents them here, reminds us that moral courage often emerges from something quieter: a sense of clarity. Silas was not confused about what he saw at Sand Creek.

His words are clear, direct, and unbearably honest. He wrote not simply as a soldier, but as a witness. And perhaps more importantly, he wrote as a human being unwilling to silence his own conscience.

There is something sacred in these letters. In an age when systemic violence was justified through layers of policy, manifest destiny, and patriotic fervor, Silas's letters cut through with the power of a single, unadorned truth: that what happened was wrong. And because it was wrong, he would not be part of it.

Nancy's presentation of Silas's letters leading up to the events of November 1864, allows us to get to know him as a person. His letters read like testimonies from a man wrestling with a brutal world, trying to hold onto a moral thread. They plead for us to ask ourselves what we might have done in his place — and what we are doing today in the face of injustice.

God Writes Straight with Crooked Lines

While reading this book, I was reminded of the phrase, "God writes straight with crooked lines." I became familiar with the saying years ago when I read it in the memoir of Father

Casimiro Roca. Father Roca was assigned to Our Lady of Peace Catholic Church in Greeley, Colorado in the early nineteen seventies. In that church years ago, he married my parents and baptized me. Father Roca would eventually be assigned to the Santuario de Chimayo in Chimayo, New Mexico — an iconic northern New Mexico adobe church where people make their own pilgrimages from across the world to gather the "holy dirt" from the base of the small church.

The phrase, which is often attributed to Saint Theresa of Avila, is a reminder that justice doesn't always emerge through a clean or direct path. History is messy, filled with contradiction and pain. Silas himself was part of a military machine that occupied Indigenous lands. And yet, within that system, he chose to resist.

We live in a time when there's no shortage of injustice. Some days it feels like we are drowning in it. And yet, stories like Silas's remind us that even in the darkest times, there are opportunities for growth, for light, and for moral clarity. Silas was a normal person — young, thoughtful, and flawed — who bore witness to horrific atrocities. The question his story poses to us is simple and devastating: What will we do when faced with the same?

Why It Matters Today

We live in a time of moral confusion. Truth is often distorted, inconvenient facts are brushed aside, and those who speak out against injustice are discredited or ignored. In such a world, the witness of Silas Soule matters more than ever.

Nancy Niero doesn't just present us with an historical narrative; she offers us a path. Silas's letters reflect not only the ethical choices of the past but also the moral dilemmas of today. In reading Silas's words, we are confronted with the same questions: Will we act when we witness injustice? Will we speak up for those who can't?

Silas did. And in doing so, he reminds us that moral courage is not limited to the exceptional. It belongs to anyone willing to see clearly and act accordingly.

Silas Soule was killed for telling the truth. But, the truth did not die with him. His letters survived. And thanks to Nancy, they will continue to live on in these pages.

I am grateful to Nancy for her work, her vision, and her courage. And, for inviting us to join her on her pilgrimage. Undoubtedly, this book is the result of deep listening, careful stewardship, and a commitment to justice.

May we, like Silas, have the courage to see clearly. May we, like Nancy, have the courage to follow the truth. And may we all remember that even in times of sadness, fear and confusion, we are never without a choice.

-Eric J. Carpio
Director, Fort Garland Museum & Cultural Center
Chief Community Museum Officer, History Colorado

Prologue:
Finding Meaning in a 30-Year Journey of Love and Loss

On November 29, 1864, a regiment of inexperienced and poorly trained Colorado soldiers attacked a peaceful camp of Cheyenne and Arapaho elders, women, and children in what is now southeast Colorado. The Cheyenne and Arapaho had been directed by the government to camp near the Big Sandy Creek, about 40 miles north of Fort Lyon. These soldiers were new recruits and their commander was a Methodist minister. After the Cheyenne and Arapaho elders, women and children were horrifically murdered these soldiers then mutilated their bodies. No one was ever held accountable for these atrocities.

Maine native Captain Silas Soule, an abolitionist and white soldier with almost three years of military experience, including fighting in battles with Confederate soldiers, tried to stop the Sand Creek Massacre from happening. He confronted military leaders the night before, standing up for what he knew were the promises of peace that had been made. His life was threatened. He disobeyed orders the following day. During the Massacre he traveled on his horse, crossing the Big Sandy many times, witnessing the ensuing violence. He saved lives by not shooting. Weeks later he wrote to his friend and colleague Major Ned Wynkoop with the horrific details of what he witnessed. He wrote to his mother with those details, as well. When the Congressional Inquiry began in February 1865, he was the first witness. His life was threatened following his testimony. He was lured out of his Denver home that he shared with his bride, Hersa, into the night of April 23. 1865 while serving as the city provost marshal. He had just gotten married only weeks earlier.

It's 3am in the urban canyon of downtown Denver where I live as I write this story that began 30 years ago. Writing this prologue is a gift to me, to reflect back on the beginnings with the act of remembrance and memory. In many ways this is the story of how to be a witness to history... marking time, discovering and solving mysteries, and finding myself in the story of a life well-lived until it was cut short... helps me to remember, and be mindful to the sacred spaces of ritual and ceremony I can create today. As people of faith, how do we be accountable today for the history that a Methodist minister led the Sand Creek Massacre? After reading this book, you, dear reader may find your ways to be a witness to Silas' life in where memory, language and journey finds you, 160 years after his death. Maybe this is your guide to discover all the many ways of creating a life of witness.

It's July, just days away from the annual gathering at the grave of Silas Soule on his birthday at historic Riverside Cemetery, the final resting place of many Black 19th century entrepreneurs like Clara Brown and Barney Ford. There are dozens of American Civil War veterans buried there and the first Jewish residents of Denver. Like so many other historic cemeteries in the American West where water continues to be a struggle for people, animals, and cemeteries, it is only rain and snow watered. It was once a beauty, but today, it is a rare occasion to find a heritage rose in bloom in the summer, planted a century ago.

This annual gathering ritual at Silas' grave, along the eastern edge of the cemetery where the silence gets interrupted frequently by trains and light rail, has been a part of summer living in Denver for me for a long time. I read his letters to everyone gathered over the course of a couple of hours. We laugh at how Silas attempts to quit smoking, we sigh at his yearning to find a wife, and we struggle to listen to the words he writes of disobeying orders and witnessing the Sand Creek Massacre where 230 Cheyenne and Arapaho elders, women, and children were horrifically murdered by Colorado soldiers in November 1864. These soldiers then mutilated the bodies, and took human remains back to Denver and parts unknown. These letters, the collection that you hold in your hand, tell the story of family, longing, struggle, despair, and sometimes, even joy, of life in America in the 19th century from the small village of Coal Creek, now known as Vinland, KS, to the mining camps of Missourie City, Black Hawk, Mountain City and Central City that he loved, to the battlefields of northern New Mexico where he helped to burn a Confederate supply train, to the Queen City of Denver and Camp Weld, to the Sand Creek Massacre on the Big Sandy Creek in southeastern Colorado.

I first learned of Silas on a new employee tour at the then Colorado History Museum, now named History Colorado, hired as a museum educator caring for the 5,000 school children who visited the museum each year. We went down the wide stairwell to the museum basement, passed the tipi around the corner, and there was a portrait of Silas in his military uniform. Young, I thought, quite young. I knew the uniform was of the American Civil War era and had known that Colorado soldiers had fought. I also knew of the Sand Creek Massacre. When I asked who this young man was, my tour guide that morning said his name for the very first time. Silas Soule, she said, and added, that he disobeyed orders to engage in the Massacre, was a witness to what happened, and then wrote a letter to a friend and colleague about what he saw. This letter, she added, forced a Congressional Inquiry in February 1865 in Denver, and then he was assassinated on the streets of Denver for speaking his truth to power. I spoke of him every opportunity I had with many of those annual 5,000 young visitors, standing at his portrait together.

A few short years later as the first executive director of the Fairmount Heritage Foundation, the historical preservation organization at Denver's two historic cemeteries, I discovered his grave, buried deep in the Grand Army of the Republic section, surrounded by fellow veterans who died of old age, as well as those who died on battle fields. I was the first person in "modern times" to have found him in 2002, but most certainly not the very first who knew where he was. My dear friend, Susie Aikman (Cherokee), shared the good news on her Sunday morning Native American music show on KUVO in Denver, CO and the rest really is history. Already in touch with Sand Creek Massacre Descendants of survivors, Susie and I were the first to host the Sand Creek Spiritual Healing Run, organized by Descendants at the grave of Silas during the run that then concluded at the State Capitol that November.

It was in these historic cemeteries where I first heard my call to ministry, went to Iliff School of Theology and then did four quarters of independent study on Silas. I wrote a biography and theological construction, in the model of using primary research sources of theological construction created by Dr. Emilie Townes in her stellar work on Ida B. Wells. I wrote a social justice play (in the Theater of the Oppressed genre) and performed the play in May 2009 during my last quarter.

I met a Silas Soule descendant at the opening of the Sand Creek Massacre National Historic Site in 2007, thanks to ancestor and beloved State Historian David Halass who introduced me to Byron Strom, the great-great nephew of Silas. Since then, I went back to school in 2019 and Silas was there too, at Phillips Theological Seminary for a Doctor of Ministry degree.

Over these 30 years, I have come to know this young man and his family well, through Byron, his military records, his mother Sophia's diary, in these letters, his testimony, and even in a 19th century family photo album. Just a few short weeks ago, I discovered, thanks to Byron, the original donation of letters to the University of Denver in the 1960s by Byron's parents, Malcolm and Edith to Dr. Raymond Carey, a beloved history professor whose hope it was to write a book about Silas.

What struck me all those years ago in the basement of a history museum and even today, is how can community find meaning making in his life, and in his death. How does community raise children to know what is right and wrong in the moment, and choose what is right? How can justice-seeking people find ways in the 21st century to make choices for the greater good around racial justice, and speaking truth to power? How can people be more like Silas in the world today?

And finally, how do people of faith remain accountable to the horrific knowledge that a Methodist minister led the Colorado soldiers at the Sand Creek Massacre to murder 230 Cheyenne and Arapaho elders, women and children camped peacefully, who then mutilated their bodies?

I ask myself these questions, and I ask these questions in community, especially in faith communities. My hope is that in this collection of letters, you find some of these answers in conversations with your family, friends, colleagues, pastors, and parishioners in the pews in your community. The most important part though, is to have the conversation...Over a meal, over a walk, over a holiday gathering, over pie and coffee, over a book study, or in any way you are in community with others. For in these conversations, we are invited to struggle with the questions and answers of meaning making.

I originally collected these 25 letters from the Western History Collection, now known as Special Collections and Archives, at the Denver Public Library, the Colorado Historical Society archives at the Stephen H. Hart Research Center, and the Military Records at the National Archives fifteen years ago. The letters from Silas to his family are in a collection that his family has cared for the last 160 years and shared with history professor Dr. Carey at the University of Denver in the 1960s. He then shared the letters to DPL and CHS. The family letters in the Anne E. Hemphill Collection have been preserved by Silas' family and are now in the care of Byron.

And a word of gentleness about these letters, especially the last three. There are words Silas uses that are not words we use in the 21st century. They are offensive and sometimes difficult to see and read on the written page. There are many details of horrific violence of Cheyenne and Arapaho elders, women, and children. Be gentle with yourself, beloved reader.

The chapters in this book have been created around the volume of letters written by Silas in each year from 1860-1865. Some chapters are fairly slim, while some chapters are larger. After thoughtful discerning, we have created two chapters from the 1864 letters, a winter-spring chapter, and a summer-fall chapter. Not only is this the year that Silas writes the most letters in this collection, but the events of 1864, from beginning to end, warrant this distinct break in the year.

I write this prologue in gratitude for Byron, Susie, David, Raymond, Gary L. Roberts, Otto Braided Hair (Northern Cheyenne), the Cheyenne and Arapaho Descendants of Sand Creek, and the many storytellers who have told Silas' story at gatherings, in churches, in ceremony, in rituals, in cemeteries, in seminaries, and in countless circles. I'm also so very grateful for the storykeepers in Byron's family of ancestors who saved the letters, the photographs, the diaries, and the photo album that all contribute to telling the story of the

Soule family and this extraordinary young man. Without these generations of Soule women who held onto and preserved these objects, and are the true storysharers, this book would never have been written.

With this book, I join a sacred gathering of many who have told his story, and I hope there will be many, many more in the future. May the storytellers of the past, now many who are ancestors, continue to be an inspiration to a new generation to tell the story, sometimes messy and complicated, of Silas and find new ways of fostering hope in a broken world.

This is my prayer... may it be so.

Chapter One
The Life of Silas Soule

He was a New England boy. His early teenage years were spent helping formerly enslaved people escape from Missouri to the Kansas Territory on the Underground Railroad. His home in Lawrence was a stop on the Railroad.[1] He came West to search for gold in the Colorado gold rush and enlisted after the American Civil War broke out. He witnessed the Sand Creek Massacre after disobeying orders to engage in the horrific violence and then wrote a letter to his influential military friend and colleague, Major Edward W. Wynkoop, telling him what he saw. He gave voice to what he witnessed at Sand Creek as the first witness in a Congressional Inquiry and a few weeks later, he was assassinated late one night on a Denver street. He had just gotten married. He had grey eyes and sandy hair and stood 5 feet 6 inches. He had premonitions of his death. He was 26 years old when he was killed.

Silas Stillman Soule was born on July 26, 1838, in Bath, ME to Amasa and Sophia Low Soule.[2] He joined brother, William Lloyd Garrison, named after Boston abolitionist William

---

1. A.B. MacDonald, "She Looks Back Seventy-Five Years to the Founding of Lawrence," *Kansas City Star*, January 13, 1929, 1.
2. *Silas Stillman Soule*, Mrs. S.B. Prentiss, presented to Kansas State Historical Society, 1924, 1.

Lloyd Garrison, and sisters Annie and Emily to complete the young Soule family.

He grew up in Maine and Massachusetts. As a teenager living in Chelsea, MA, his mother read out loud to her family excerpts of *Uncle Tom's Cabin* by Harriet Beecher Stowe, published in *The National Era*, a Boston newspaper in 1852. Silas' sister remembered that the young Soule family gathered in the parlor every Sunday afternoon listening to the words of Black families destroyed by enslavement in the South. The words of Stowe who described the horrors of living in the South for men, women, and children of African descent, inspired Amasa to join the New England Emigration Aid Company and move to the Kansas Territory. By the mid-1850s, much of New England was in deep debate over the abolitionist movement and the cause of freedom for enslaved people. Men like Horace Greeley and Henry Ward Beecher (Harriet's father) were calling on New Englanders to help resist the spread of enslavement. Inspired by this call, many New Englanders became deeply involved in the creation of the Underground Railroad. Several historians believe that emigrant companies from New England were established to travel to the Midwest to set up "stops" on the Railroad to give passage through the Midwest and into Canada to formerly enslaved people. Others believe the work of the emigrant companies was to settle the Kansas Territory and bring it into the Union as a free state. The New England Emigrant Aid Company was part of the wave of New Englanders who traveled in 1854 to Kansas to be part of "doing something to put a quick stop to the onward march of the slave power."[3] The Soule family was deeply committed to the movement.

Amasa Soule and his son, William left from Boston on the journey West traveling with the New England Emigrant Com-

---

3. *A Little Satire on Emigrant Aid, Amasa Soule and the Descandum Kansas Improvement Company*, Kansas Historical Quarterly, Russell K. Hickman, November 193 (vol. 8, No. 4), 342-349.

pany. They arrived in Lawrence on November 22. Lawrence, which later became the hotbed for the Kansas abolitionist movement, then consisted of 50 shacks and offered poor accommodation to the new arrivals. The Soule men took out a claim near Coal Creek, near present day Vinland, KS, built a log cabin, and were joined by the rest of the family, including Silas, in October 1855.[4]

"My brother, Silas and Brown (abolitionist, John Brown) were close friends. Silas was out on many a foray with him. I recall well when Brown came to our cabin one night with thirteen slaves, men, women and children. He had run them away from Missouri. Brown left them with us. Father would always take in all the Negroes he could. Silas took the whole thirteen from our home eight miles to Mr. Grover's stone barn, two miles west of where the Haskell Indian school is now. The Negroes stayed there, hidden in the barn for several days, when a chance offered and they were taken still further toward freedom by another agent of the Underground. At the tender young age of 17, Silas was escorting formerly enslaved people from the Missouri Territory on a journey of freedom with abolitionist John Brown. Their family home was a station on the Underground Railroad."[5]

Just a few years later, Silas and several other Lawrence men found themselves immersed in what would later become a major event in the history of the Underground Railroad in Kansas Territory. Dr. John Doy, the general conductor of the Railroad in Lawrence was arrested in Missouri in January 1859 while conducting 13 formerly enslaved people to freedom. In a plot that took several months to develop, Silas arrived in July at the St. Joseph, MO jail with a group of men from Lawrence, pretending to be drunk. He was arrested and was incarcerated in the same jail as Doy. He convinced the jail keeper that he had a message from Doy's wife. The note,

---
4. *Silas Stillman Soule.*
5. *She Looks Back*, 1.

in fact, read "Tonight at twelve o'clock." Later that night, the Lawrence men overpowered the jailer, freed Doy, and led him across the Missouri River and back into Kansas.[6] When they reached Lawrence, a photo was taken of "The Immortal Ten," and a huge copy of the photo hung in the Kansas State Historical Society in Topeka, KS when I first visited. Doy's capture and rescue was publicized nationally and brought wide support to the movement in Kansas.

In October 1859, abolitionist John Brown from Osawatomie, Kansas Territory, and 21 followers, including two sons of Frederick Douglas, arrived in Harpers Ferry, WV on October 16, 1859, hoping to spark a rebellion of freed slaves and lead an "army of emancipation" to dismantle the institution of enslavement. They took 60 prominent hostages, seized the United States arsenal and its rifle works, and were captured within days.

Brown was executed in Charles Town, WV on December 2, 1859. Silas was asked by Boston abolitionists to come to Harrisburg, PA in February 1860 as part of a reconnaissance to help two of Brown's Raiders, who had been captured, escape from jail in Charles Town. The first letter written in this collection is written from Harrisburg. Aaron Stevens had traveled with Brown since 1856.[7] He had been captured and was imprisoned in the same jail cell as Brown. Albert Hazlett was another one of Brown's loyal followers.[8] He was also captured and in the same jail cell as Stevens. The attempt to break them out of jail was abandoned because of snow on the ground and there was no way of rescuing the prisoners as they would be tracked. Hazlett and Stevens also felt that a jail break would put their jailer, the same jailer who cared for John Brown in

---

6. *She Looks Back*, 1.
7. David S. Reynolds, *John Brown Abolitionist, The Man Who Killed Slavery, Sparked the Civil War, and Seeded Civil Rights* (New York, NY, Knopf, 2005), 256.
8. Reynolds, 277.

his final days, in peril. Stevens and Hazlett were executed in March 1860

Sometime that spring, Silas traveled to Boston where the abolition movement was thriving, and he was feted by abolitionist leadership. He met Walt Whitman. He spent time with William Wilde Thayer and Charles W. Eldridge, the publishers of Whitman's third edition of *Leaves of Grass*, and Richard J. Hinton, a Kansas abolitionist. In one of his early letters, Silas wrote to Thayer, Eldridge and Hinton after his return home to Coal Creek and announces that he's heading to the gold fields of Colorado with his brother and cousin.

Silas' letters from Gilpin County are filled with the details of claims, hard rock mining, his work as a blacksmith and making only enough money for grub (food!). It's in these first letters in the summer of 1861 that he longs to be back in Kansas Territory.

The American Civil War erupted in April 1861 and the Colorado Territory quickly responded to the outbreak. Territorial Governor William Gilpin raised the First Colorado Regiment of Volunteers to combat a potential threat by Confederates to the gold fields. Silas enlisted in Company K, First Regiment, in the Colorado Infantry on December 11, 1861, under the command of Captain Samuel Robbins.

The regiment left Denver in late February 1862 headed for Fort Union, NM as reports were heard of Confederate General Henry Sibley's win at the Battle of Valverde in southern New Mexico near Fort Craig. Silas described in detail of the Great March from Camp Weld to Fort Union, marching 350 miles in 14 days. The regiment, under the command of Colonel John Slough, confronted Confederate troops on March 26 at Glorietta Pass in New Mexico and a battle erupted. Silas, under the command of Major John Chivington, fought at Johnson's Ranch where the men came upon a

Confederate supply train, burned it and killed a Confederate chaplain. With provisions gone, the Confederates slowly retreated from Northern New Mexico and made their way back to Texas after a brief skirmish at the Battle of Peralta. Slough resigned his command following the Battle at Glorieta Pass and was replaced by former Methodist minister, now promoted to Colonel, John Chivington.[9]

In a letter to his sister Emily on September 4, 1863, Silas wrote of his deep concern for the safety of his family following Quantrill's Raid on Lawrence on August 21, 1863 where pro-enslavement Missourians raided Lawrence, destroyed the town, and murdered 150 men and boys.[10] He wrote, "I received your letter last night and was very glad to hear that you had all come out safe, for I was very much afraid Bill would go up the flume. I think you were all in luck, I am sorry that I have no money, but I will borrow $50 and send it. I want to go back there, but don't see much chance now."

He offered sympathy to his sister, wished he was there to help, and asked that his mother be brave. He was also deeply concerned about the loss of the city of Lawrence, and to his neighbors. Lawrence men were specifically targeted in the raid and Silas' concern for the safety of his brother, Bill was of particular concern.

By October 1863, Silas was appointed as a recruiter for the 1st Colorado Regiment. He was promoted to the rank of Captain but complained to his sister Annie in a letter that although his pay was a little bit better than it was before, "I believe I will spend it as fast as I get it for fear it will get burned up if I try to save any."

---

9. Byron Parker, interview with author, Pecos, NM, September 23, 2024.
10. Civil War Timeline, National Park Service, accessed on December 20, 2024, https://www.nps.gov/gett/learn/historyculture/civil-war-timeline.htm.

The first letter in his military records from the National Archives is written to Chivington on January 3, 1864, from Fort Garland. He wrote that he had procured a mule and rode all night in snow that was deep and the weather cold, with no trail to follow. "Suffered considerably," he wrote. "You can have some idea of my trip over the range the snow was fifteen foot deep in some places and wind blowing snow so I could hardly see feet ahead of me."

"I got frost bit a little none to hurt though now I suppose you are tired of reading this report. I will come to business," he wrote. He then proceeded to tell Chivington of the current reenlisting problems at Fort Garland, caused by one obstinate lieutenant. He left the next day heading to Conejos in southern Colorado Territory, near the New Mexico border.

He is back and forth between Conejos and Fort Garland and writes to his mom in February 1864 that he is hopeful that he would receive a lieutenant colonel's commission (which never materialized) and that he would like to travel to the Idaho Territory to assist in raising a new regiment (which also never materialized). He also wrote in this letter that if he didn't go to Idaho, he hoped to get a furlough in the spring to visit her (which didn't materialize).

He wrote Chivington in February 1864 from Fort Garland about his success and challenges in reenlisting men to continue their service in the military.

Denverites woke up to another day of rain on May 19, 1864, but it soon became one of the most dangerous and deadliest days in the young city's history when Cherry Creek flooded over its banks and caused major flooding in the center of the city.[11] In a letter to his mother on June 2, 1864, Silas wrote

---

11. Brian K. Trembath, "May 1864 Brought Denver's First Big Flood – and Swept Away Much More," Denver Public Library, May 20, 2020, accessed December 20, 2024, https://history.denverlibrary.org/news/denver-may-

about being at the flood. He wrote, "Have been busy for the last month fixing up my papers and just as I got them fixed my office was swept away by the flood and I lost everything I had – papers, letters, clothing, and all – wasn't I in luck? Blessed are the poor for they have nothing to lose!" He wrote to his sister that the flood tore down churches, printing offices and it washed away about a quarter of the city. In the summer of 1864, Silas and his newly assigned Company D are on the move again, this time to Fort Lyon, located on the Arkansas River in southeastern Colorado. He is in command of 94 men. In a letter to his sister Annie, he predicts that he will soon have some "Indian fighting to do." He ends this letter with what could be the first mention that he is thinking about marriage. "I think I shall go to Maine to marry so if you see any nice girl who wants to be the wife of a Captain of a hundred braves tell them that I am the man they are looking for." He never got back to Maine.

The summer of 1864 is filled with several letters written by Silas to his family from Fort Lyon. In one of the only references, he makes in this collection of letters, he responds to what has apparently been written by his mother and sister about his lack of acting like a Christian man. He responds in a letter to his sister in July 1864 with, "you and mother write for me to be a Cristian [sic] and not wild &c., but the Army don't improve a fellow much in that respect and you know I never was much of a Christian, and am naturally wild, but I have seen so much of the world and are not much changed. I think there is not much danger of my spoiling – our Col. is a Methodist Preacher and whenever he sees me drinking, gambling, stealing, or murdering he says, he will write to Mother or my sister Annie, so I have to go straight."

Silas spent all summer at Fort Lyon. He wrote his mother in July, "I suppose you think I spend a good deal of money, but

---

1864-brought-denvers-first-big-flood%E2%80%94and-swept-away-much-more history when you consider that it costs sixty dollars for a coat, twenty for a pair of pants, sixteen for a pair of boots, ten for a coat, and six and a half a piece for shirts, it counts up and you know a captain has to wear good clothes. I had a birthday on the 26th, I suppose you know. I am 26 years old, most old enough to marry, ain't I?"

In June, Nathan Hungate, his wife, and two children were murdered 35 miles south of Denver. Their bodies were brought to the Queen City and placed on display at a theatre for viewing. Historians suggest that the Hungate murders heralded a more intensified attack on the Cheyenne and Arapaho.

Many of the news reports in the summer of 1864 demonstrate that Denverites were in fear of an attack by the Cheyenne and Arapaho. All of this fear can be attributed to the influence of Chivington and John Evans, territorial governor and also acting superintendent of Indian Affairs. *Rocky Mountain News* Founder and Editor William Byers also helped in fanning the flames of fear by publishing editorials blasting the Cheyenne and Arapaho in his newspaper. A proclamation sent out in the beginning of the summer of 1864 by Evans, had commanded all "Friendly" Native Americans of the Cheyenne and Arapaho to go to Fort Lyon to receive supplies and to find safety. This was contrary to the standing order at all forts within the Colorado Territory that all members of the military should shoot and kill any Native American that approached a fort.[12] Southern Cheyenne Chief Black Kettle and Southern Arapaho Chief Left Hand later told Major Edward Wynkoop and Lt. Joseph Cramer, that tribes tried several times to contact the posts at Fort Lyon to accept Evan's offer, but the sentries would not allow them to approach in some instances even fired on them.[13]

---

12. Sand Creek Massacre, National Park Service, accessed December 19, 2024, https://www.nps.gov/sand/index.htm
13. Report of the John Evans Study Committee, Northwestern University, University Relations, May 2014, Evanston, IL, 65.

By the end of the summer several Cheyenne Indian chiefs, camped near Smokey Hill River, sent word to Wynkoop, post commander at Fort Lyon (and Silas' immediate commander) that they had several white captives and were willing to return them to the military. And Black Kettle requested a peace council. Wynkoop and Silas traveled to the camp, along with 126 soldiers, took the captives and upon their return to Fort Lyon, Wynkoop and Silas escorted a number of Cheyenne and Arapaho chiefs to visit Denver in mid-September for the purpose of meeting with Evans and Chivington to work towards peace.

After much refusal to see the chiefs, Evans finally agreed, only after Wynkoop insisted, and the Camp Weld Council convened on September 28, 1864. It is in testimony of that event that we read that Evans refused to make peace with the Cheyenne and Arapaho, and instead stated to Southern Cheyenne Chief White Antelope that whatever peace the tribes want to make, must be with the military authorities, and not with him. He seemed to assure the Cheyenne and Arapaho chiefs that they and their followers would be safe if they did as his earlier plan prescribed and sought refuge at Fort Lyon, which they did.[14] Wynkoop and Silas escorted the chiefs back to Fort Lyon and the chiefs returned to their people. And within days, Wynkoop reported to Major General Samuel Curtis, commander of the Department of Kansas that he was going to allow some of the Cheyenne and Arapaho, camped peacefully at the post to receive rations.

Summer moved into fall and Silas wrote in October that he hoped to get a furlough and head to Maine to visit his sister Annie in early 1865 (which never materialized). He also wrote Chivington in October asking to have orders sent to him at Fort Lyon so that he could start mustering out his Company of men. He needed to make a trip to Denver to retrieve papers

---

14. Report of the John Evans Study, 58.

that he thought had already been sent to him, but he had not yet received. He signed this letter with "I am with much respect, your obedient servant, Silas S. Soule." He didn't get those orders to go to Denver.

On November 2, 1864, Wynkoop was relieved of his command and assigned to the headquarters of the District of the Upper Arkansas at Fort Riley, Kansas Territory. Before he left Fort Lyon on November 26, he joined Major Scott Anthony, who replaced him, and Black Kettle, who brought the Cheyenne people to the fort, for a council. It is at that council that Anthony told Black Kettle and the Cheyenne people to give up their arms and camp with the Arapaho on Sand Creek, located 40 miles from Fort Lyon. At his testimony later in February 1865, Silas mentioned that it was he who first came upon soldiers on the evening of November 27, ten or twelve companies of 100-Day volunteers. He and Chivington talked about the location where the Arapaho and Cheyenne were camped. Silas told him that there were some Indians camped near the fort, below Fort Lyon, but they were not dangerous.

Chivington and the regiment camped near Fort Lyon that night. It was the following day, November 28, that Silas was ordered by Major Anthony to join Chivington's command that very night, with three days cooked rations and twenty uncooked. By that evening, Silas had been told that Chivington was going to attack Black Kettle's camp the following day. He tried desperately to relay information about the peaceful relations that existed between the officers at Fort Lyon and the Cheyenne and Arapahoe to Chivington, speaking to Major Anthony. It was in that conversation that Silas said he was protesting against attacking the camps.

Again, in his testimony, Silas stated that Major Anthony indicated that the regiment was going to the Smoky Hill "to fight the hostile Indians; he also said that he was in for killing all Indians, and that he was only acting or had been only acting friendly with them until he could get a force large enough to go out and kill all the Indians."[15] In that conversation, Silas reminded him of the pledges the soldiers had made to the Cheyenne and Arapaho.

Silas travelled with the regiment throughout the night and arrived at the village of the Cheyenne and Arapaho just before sunrise.

On November 29, Cheyenne and Arapaho women, children and elders, were attacked in their camps at dawn. In the seven-hour Massacre, 230 Cheyenne and Arapaho elders, women and children were brutally killed that day by soldiers under Chivington's command.

In a letter to Wynkoop on December 14, 1864 Silas described the Massacre in great detail and then wrote, "The massacre lasted six or eight hours, and a good many Indians escaped. I tell you Ned it was hard to see little children on their knees, have their brains beat out by men professing to be civilized. One Squaw was wounded, and a fellow took a hatchet to finish her, she held her arms up to defend her, and he cut one arm off, and held the other with one hand, and dashed the hatchet through her brain."

On December 18, Silas wrote to his mother with the first mention of the Massacre. He wrote, "I was present at a Massacre of three hundred Indians, mostly women and children. (In a letter dated January 8, 1865, he clarifies that the death count was closer to 130 women and children killed. And all of them scalped). It was a horrable (sic) scene and I would not let my Company fire. They were friendly and some of our soldiers were in their Camp at the time trading. It looked too hard for me to see little Children on their knees begging for their lives, have their brains beat out like dogs. It was a Rega-

---

15. Report of the Secretary of War, Silas Soule Testimony, February 16, 1864, 13.

ment (sic) of 100 days men who acomplished (sic) the noble deed. Some of the Indians fought when they saw no chance of escape and killed twelve and wounded forty of our men." Before signing off he wrote that he still had hopes that he would visit Maine during the winter, but maybe not until the spring. He ends this letter with, "Don't get worried for there is not the least danger in the world of my getting killed, and as I am the most interested party, you shouldn't fret."

Silas started the New Year by counting dead bodies on the Massacre ground on New Year's Day. In January 1865, he and his regiment were mustered out of service. The officers were relieved of duty, and according to a letter to his mother written January 8 from Ft. Lyon, Silas was trying to assemble all of his papers, so he could "start for the States right off." As many of his fellow officers suspected, Silas was appointed to the veteran battalion of the First Colorado Cavalry and named as provost marshal general of the District of Colorado and never did return to "the States."

"I hope the authorities at Washington will investigate the killing of those Indians. I think they will be apt to hoist some of our high officials. I would not fire on the Indians with my Co. and the Col. said he would have me cashiered, but he is out of the service before me and I think I stand better than he does in regard to his great Indian fight," he wrote in the January letter, the last known letter written to his mother. He concludes this letter with "I am reforming in regard to my bad habits, Mother, for I have left off chewing tobacco and smoking a pipe, but I will smoke cigars when I can get them. I don't drink, so you see I am getting quite respectable and will stand a chance of getting a wife when I go down east."

Chivington resigned his commission in January 1865.

True to Silas' hope, there was an investigation of the Sand Creek Massacre. An inquiry convened on February 9 to investigate the conduct of Chivington during the months of October through December 1864. The commission was made up of Lt. Col. Samuel F. Tappan, Captain Ed. A. Jacobs, and Captain George H. Stilwell, all of the veteran battalion, First Colorado Cavalry. The first witness was Silas.[16]

In his testimony, Silas said at Sand Creek that he witnessed Indians advancing toward Chivington's command with their hands up. He stated that no advance warning had been given to the camp of the subsequent attack. "Were the woman and children shot while attempting to escape from Colonel Chivington's command," Silas was asked. "They were," he answered. "Were the women and children followed while attempting to escape, shot down and scalped, and otherwise mutilated, by any of Colonel Chivington's command? They were." Were any efforts made by the commanding officers, Colonels Chivington, Shoup, and Major Anthony, to prevent these mutilations? Not that I know of," was his answer.

Just a few weeks after giving his testimony Silas married Hersa A. Coberly on April 1, officiated by J.H. Kehler, a former rector at St. John's Church in Denver, and the chaplain of the First Colorado Cavalry Regiment.

On the evening of Sunday, April 23, 1865, just three weeks after his wedding, Silas returned home late one evening with Hersa, when shots rang out and as provost marshal of the city, he immediately responded. He came to the intersection of 15th and Lawrence Streets and was assassinated by an assailant who had drawn him from his home.

Here is how the *Rocky Mountain News* reported his death the following day... "Our city was thrown into a feverish excitement last evening by the assassination of Captain S. S. Soule of the Colorado First. The sad affair took place about half past ten o'clock, and was evidently coolly and deliberately

---

16. Silas Soule Testimony, February 12, 1865, 8.

planned, and as systematically carried out. For some time past the Captain had been in charge of the Provost Guard of the city and neighborhood and his duties in that capacity had, as a natural consequence, arrested many enemies.

"Threats against his life have been freely and frequently made so we are informed and no longer ago, than yesterday he said that he was expecting to be attacked. In the evening he and his wife were visiting at the house of a friend and returned home between nine and ten o'clock. Shortly after a number of pistol shots were fired in the upper part of the city, evidently to decoy him out and the Captain started to ascertain the cause. Whilst passing along Lawrence street near F, and directly in front of the residence of Dr. Cunningham, he seems to have been met by the assassin, and the indications are that both fired at the same instant, or near together that the reports seemed simultaneous. Probably the Captain, expecting to be attacked was in readiness and when the other man presented his pistol, he did the same, but the intended assassin fired an instant sooner and with but too fatal effect. The ball entered the Captain's face at the point of the right cheek bone, passing backward and upward and lodging in the back part of the head. He fell back dead appearing not to have moved a muscle after falling. The other man, from the indications, was wounded in the right hand or arm how severely is not known. His pistol was dropped at the scene and he immediately started and ran toward the military camp in the upper part of the city leaving a distinct trail of blood where he passed along. When the shots were fired they were standing four feet apart, face to face.

"Within less than a minute after the fatal shot, one of the provost guards and Mr. Ruter reached the spot. The Captain was already dead and his murderer had disappeared. They informed Dr. Cummingham and a guard was sent for. A number of persons, soldiers and civilians soon gathered around and after a few minutes the body was removed to the building occupied by the offices of the headquarters of the District.

"The excitement this morning when the facts became generally known was intense. Hundreds of citizens visited the scene of the tragedy, and it has formed the burthon of conversations throughout the city all day. Patrols were dispatched in every direction and it is hardly possible that he will escape more than for a day or two. Probably he will be overtaken today. Of his identity we shall at present refrain from speaking though there is scarce doubt, but it is clearly known. The cause is said to have grown out of an arrest by the Captain in the discharge of his duty as Provost Marshall. Captain Soule was highly respected by his brother officers, and beloved by the men of his company. He was married in this city on the 1st last and consequently leaves a young wife to mourn his terrible and untimely fate."[17]

The commission still investigating John Chivington and his actions at Sand Creek adjourned early that day to help in making arrangements for Silas' funeral the following morning.

In the same column as the funeral announcement published in the *Rocky Mountain News*, on the next day, a small note announced that "Mr. B.L. Ford of the People's Restaurant was having a big ball and festival at his place on the evening of April 25 in commemoration of the fall of Richmond and the downfall of human slavery in the south." Barney Ford, formerly enslaved and who had been transported on the Underground Railroad to freedom, became a wealthy proprietor of several well-known hotels and restaurants in Denver during the 1860s.[18]

---

17. *Rocky Mountain News*, April 24, 1865, 1.
18. *Rocky Mountain News*, April 25, 1865, 1.

At Silas's funeral on April 25, Reverend H.H. Hitchings, preached the funeral sermon and said, "He had no fear of work, of fatigue, of suffering, of death.

"He discharged his duty well as Provost Marshall of this city; he went on his way when he knew that the alarm that called him might be only to decoy him into danger. He knew that his life had been threatened and that five shots had been sent at him with deadly intent. He did his duty in the midst of danger and of death; he fell by an assassin's bullet. He had great moral strength, fortitude, strong convictions, honesty of purpose. He was physically and morally brave."

The *Rocky Mountain News* reported that there was a long line of carriages. – almost all of the public and private ones in town were in the citizen's cortege in a procession from the church.[19] Men from Silas' company, chaplains, a governor, and hundreds of citizens all made their way from the church to Mount Prospect Cemetery where Silas was buried. A card of thanks was published in the *Rocky Mountain News* by Hersa on June 19, 1866 a year after his burial saying, "the undersigned takes this method of extending her heartfelt thanks to the officers and members of the First Colorado, and all the others, who have so kindly and thoughtfully placed the beautiful and enduring monument over the remains of her deceased husband, Capt. Silas S. Soule. She begs them all to believe that this mark of their esteem for the dead is a solace to her mourning heart, and will ever be remembered with gratitude by her."[20]

Almost two weeks later in testimony before the inquiry, George F. Price, captain of the Second Colorado Cavalry, gave testimony of a conversation he had had with Silas earlier that spring in March as they were riding in a buggy from Denver to Central City. He said, "In a conversation on that occasion,

---

19. *Rocky Mountain News*, April 27, 1865, 1.
20. *Rocky Mountain News*, June 19, 1866, 4.

Silas referred to the affair at Sand Creek, and the nature of his testimony about it; that he fully expected to be killed on account of that testimony; that he was also fully satisfied, after they had killed him, his character would be assailed, and an attempt made to destroy his testimony before a certain commission instructed to take testimony concerning the said Sand Creek Affair."[21] Indeed Silas' premonition about his own death, and the subsequent barrage to his character was why Price testified in the inquiry.

His mom, the recipient of so many of the letters he wrote, found out about his death in a letter she received on May 9, and then wrote in her diary on May 10, "don't know what to do with myself."[22]

In a general order on June 22, 1867, Silas was posthumously promoted to the rank of major for "faithful and meritorious services."[23] His remains were disinterred from the cemetery, along with thousands of others, when it was converted to eventually become Cheesman Park and the Denver Botanic Gardens. He was reinterred at Riverside Cemetery in Denver, in the Grand Army of the Republic block which was originally purchased by American Civil War veterans.

The majestic white marble monument that Denver citizens had helped pay for, did not come to Riverside with him.

The assassin, Charles W. Squires, an unassigned recruit in the 2nd Regiment Colorado Cavalry, was arrested a few months later. At his October 1865 trial, he was charged with murder and desertion. He was never held accountable for the murder.[24]

---

21. George F. Price Testimony, 189.
22. Sophia Low Soule diary, 1865, Anne E. Hemphill Collection.
23. Silas Soule, Military Records.
24. Squires died on December 9, 1869 from gangrene in New York. Email from Gary L. Roberts, May 20, 2025.

Chapter Two
The Letters, 1860 – Leaving Kansas

The first letter in this chapter is written by Silas from Harrisburg, PA where he had quickly traveled from Kansas Territory, along with fellow Kansans John Montgomery, and "Carpenter, Rice, Gardner, and Willis," at the request of Boston abolitionist Richard J. Hinton.[1] He was asked to do reconnaissance and help break out two of John Brown's Harpers Ferry Raiders, Aaron D. Stevens and Albert Hazlett, who had been captured and imprisoned in the same Charleston jail that John Brown had been in. The breakout ultimately failed due to a snow fall, where tracks would have obviously led authorities to discover everyone involved. Both Hazlett and Stevens resisted the escape once Silas, who was arrested to get into the jail to meet with the men, described the plan. In the second letter, Silas has just returned from meeting these three Boston abolitionists, William Wilde Thayer, Charles W. Eldridge and Richard J. Hinton and poet Walt Whitman, who is about to publish the third edition of *Leaves of Grass* with his new publishing firm, Thayer and Eldridge.

---

1. Thomas Wentworth Higginson, *Cheerful Yesterdays: The American Negro, His History and Literature* (New York, NY: Arno Press, 1968), 233.

Letter One
to George Cutter, friend

Feb 21st,1860
Harrisburg, Pennsylvania

Friend George

I suppose you would like to know how things are progressing in this civilized country. I left Pittsburg Sunday night and arrived here Monday morning and am stopping at the drover house on the bank of the Susquehannah. Harrisburg is a pretty town. Everything looks clean and neat. The state legislature is in session now, and there are a good many people here. There is about a foot of snow on the ground and splendid Sleighing and the way the crinoline is flying is a caution.

I was up to the theater last night. They played a piece called the Harrisburg Fireman. They done pretty well. It seems good to hear a band of good music and see all sorts of Amusements once more, and I believe in getting all the enjoyment I can while I have a chance. I went to a performance in Pittsburg last Saturday night and when the curtain arrose [sic] you never heard such a noise in your life. There were about 500 Boys in the house and a harder set never lived. They drove the actors from the stage and broke everything to pieces. They broke all the windows out and threw the seats down from the third tier and raised the old scratch generally Well, enough of this.

It is so dark that I cannot see the lines. This snow is a bad thing for us. We cannot do much until it goes off. The boys are here with the exception of two. One has gone to New York and the other is looking about among the Quackers [sic] , and I am going to start for Harpers ferry and Charlestown to look for work.

 I shall not be back for a week so this is the last letter that any of you will get untill [sic] I get back. Tell Father that I wrote to him yesterday. I did not tell that I was going away and you need not, for he might worry. I don't know wheather [sic] the folks know where I am, but I suppose they susspect [sic] something is up. Tell father that I am in this place and may not go back for a month. I owe McQuestin a days work and two with the team. If I don't go back tell him to take it out of any thing he can find that belongs to me. I believe that I don't owe much there any how. Give my love to every body, your folks in particular. I would like to hear what kind of a time they had to the festival etc. etc.

Well, be a good Boy and tell Alf, Barnes, Will, McQ. and every body else to do the same.

And remember
S. Stillman

I sent a little note in this to Charlotte. Don't you open it.

-Anne E. Hemphill Collection

***

To set the stage for this letter, one has to return to Charlestown, WV and the execution of abolitionist John Brown in December 1859. Brown, who proclaimed he had been called by God to dismantle the system of enslavement, had been captured, charged, and convicted of treason for leading the Harpers Ferry raid in October. He had been in conversation with Frederick Douglas and Harriet Tubman in the years prior to the Raid about his calling. Brown and Douglass met for the last time in August where after hearing the details of the Raid, Douglass declined to join Brown. Douglass later called John Brown "a brave and glorious man...History has no better illustration of pure, disinterested benevolence."[2]

Silas was one of several men who was quickly summoned in early February 1860 to Harrisburg from Lawrence by abolitionist Richard H. Hinton and Unitarian minister Rev. T.W. Higginson, the latter who was partially funding the breakout of Aaron D. Stevens and Albert Hazlett. According to the Coal Creek Library minutes of December 1859, Silas' name had been added to the committee for planning a Valentine's Day Festival.[3] I suspect that he would have attended, if he hadn't been unexpectedly requested to travel to Harrisburg.

Silas' letter to his old friend George Cutter, who was a Vinland, Kansas Territory neighbor from their teen years, has some nuggets that point to George knowing more details of Silas' plans than words illustrate. "This snow is a bad thing for us," he writes to George. Ultimately, snow becomes one of the two reasons that the attempt to break Stevens and Hazlett out of jail in Charlestown, fails. The other reason is that after Silas gets arrested and is placed in the same jail, to break them out, they resist him saying that they would fear for the safety of the jailer, Avis, who had also cared for John Brown in the same jail.[4]

The other nugget that demonstrates that we readers need to read between the lines is, "I am going to start for Harpers ferry [sic] and Charlestown to look for work." We clearly know the work is to break Stevens and Hazlett out of jail.

George and Silas were not only great friends and neighbors, but they were also abolitionists together too. George

---

2. Frederick Douglass National Historic Site, Facebook page, accessed May 21, 2025.
3. Byron Strom, phone interview with author, September 13, 2024.
4. Higginson, *Cheerful Yesterdays*, 234.

arrived in eastern Kansas in "March 1856 ready to fight for a free Kansas."[5] George fought with Frederick Brown, one of John Brown's sons, at the Battle of Osawatomie in August 1856 near Osawatomie, Kansas Territory where young Brown was killed and where George was shot several times, "lucky to survive with just a limp for the rest of his life."

This first letter in the collection gives us a glimpse of letters to come about who Silas was in the early 1860s. We read in this letter, and many more to come, even the next letter, of the details of his travels. He's illustrating them for us to follow and in some cases to return to. He's attentive to the weather. He tells a story, with the details of what matters most to him. This first letter sets the stage, love of family and friends, speaking out for justice with fellow abolitionists who put their lives at risk together as a band of brothers would.

And not just speaking up for justice but showing up for justice. Traveling to Harrisburg, PA was not a simple journey, but a complicated one. This moral arc of justice is already being developed as he is surrounded by others in a community, beginning in Kansas with abolitionists like John Brown and friends like George Cutter, and in this call to action in Harrisburg, PA. We will see in these letters to come that his moral foundations of what is right from wrong, gets challenged or exposed, in the Colorado Territory when he is confronted with injustice in the ranks of military, in negotiations for peace with the Cheyenne and Arapaho, and in what he says and does in his attempts to stop the Sand Creek Massacre from happening the night before, and then disobeying orders the next day.

---

5. "Charlotte Varnum Cutter's Civil War," "Civil War Quilts-Quilts," and "Women's History Focusing on the American Civil War," by Barbara Brackman, accessed September 18, 2021, https://civilwarquilts.blogspot.com/2021/09/charlotte-varnum-cutters-civil-war.html.

The essence of what this 22-year-old knows of right from wrong begins here in the words of this first letter. You may ask, how does he know the moral arc of right from wrong at such a young age? I hope by the end of this book, you will discover all the answers to that sacred question.

***

Letter Two
to William Thayer, Charles Eldridge, and Richard J. Hinton

May 9th, 1860
Coal Creek, Kansas

Dear Sirs,

I arrived here last Fryday [sic]. I left Boston Thursday night for Stonington. There I took the boat for New York, left there Fryday [sic] morning, arrived in Phila[delphia] that noon and had to wait until six before I could get of[f] and then had to go with a cargo of Emigrants that talked beautiful Dutch. We didn't get to Pittsburg until Sunday. It was an awful journey. If it wasn't for some girls that had some get up to them I don't know what I should have done. As it was we had an amusing time. We crossed the alleghanies [sic] Saturday. If I had been in a hurry I should have walked. As it was we walked some of the time and waited for the cars and pushed going uphill. Pittsburg is as dirty as ever. I went over to the coal mines and passed off for a coal merchant and was put through in fine style. I distributed the cards of Thayer and Eldridge all through Ohio and Indiana as long as they lasted. I went to St. Louis and got on the boat and took deck passage to Hannibal then the cars to Atchison, Boat to Leavenworth and stage to Lawrence. Tell Walt [Whitman] that when he wants to get up another book and thinks he has seen all the world he must take a second-class ticket to Kansas and I think it would be very appropriate to name it after a weed called Smart weed alaias [sic] Ass Smart. Tell Walt that I have a good deal to say about him and when he comes out here the folks will treat him well.

Now I must tell you something that will surprise you. When I arrived here I found a party waiting for me to go to pikes peak. My Brother and cousin were in the gang going with a quartz machine belonging to Solomon and Parker of Lawrence and there was no way but I must go. They started yesterday. I am to start tomorrow and overtake them. I had not time to go [to] Ms so I went to Stewart and told him every thing. He is all right. He brought up three head the other night making sixty-eight since he commenced. He met with a mishap yesterday.

I went with him to Lawrence in the morning and we had not been there more than an hour before a runner came in with word that his place had been attacked and one man taken and one wounded. We started off as quick as possible but could only raise four horsemen and by the time we got our arms they were off a good way. We followed them about six miles but found that they all had good horses and were so far ahead that we could not overtake them. When last seen they were going it with a boy on behind one of them. He was calling for assistance and one of them beating him with a club to keep him quiet. He was a free boy that has been here for two years. They were plowing in the field and had revolvers but there were five of the kidnappers. There were fifteen or twenty shots fired and one only was wounded that he know of. He was shot in the hip. The ball went out and didn't damage him much. Things look kind of blue and some one will be shot before long. It is supposed hurd was one of them. I gave S those letters to give to M as will see him as soon as any body and I told him just how things stand. He is the man. I hope you will write to him. He don't like G's actions very well. Stearns and another man that I was not acquainted with arrived monday. Stearns went to G's before we got over. I have posted S about Stearns and if they get ahead of him they will have to get up early. He is going to make a haul of about fifteen next week. He talked with G but couldn't get him to go. I can't write anymore. Give my love to all. Tell Walt to send that Book to me. Direct to S Soule, Lawrence Ks Box 43.

John E. Stewart – if you write to him maybe you had better put it inside of another envelope and direct it to Amasa Soule box 43.

S.S. Soule
I am afraid that G is not worth a damn.

-Richard J. Hinton Manuscript Collection
Kansas State Historical Society

***

This letter, and many others to come, demonstrate the immeasurable delight of the details of travel and daily life, containing some big feelings and hopes for the future that we will read again and again in future letters. It's written from Coal Creek, which is present day Vinland, KS, located a few miles south of Lawrence, and the then home of the Soules.

He has just returned from a bit of a whirlwind unexpected trip to Harrisburg, PA in February. He then travels to Boston to meet with two new friends, William Wilde Thayer and Charles Eldridge, who are the publishers of Walt Whitman's third edition of *Leaves of Grass*, and the poet himself, Walt Whitman. In addition to Thayer and Eldridge, Silas writes to Richard J. Hinton, who is also an abolitionist. Hinton, who had moved to Kansas Territory with the New England Emigrant Company, was the one who sent for Silas' help to break out Aaron Stevens and Albert Hazlett from the jail in Charlestown, WV earlier in the year. The attempt was unsuccessful, and both men were executed on March 16.

The 21st century expert of the Walt Whitman Archives, Dr. Kenneth Price, professor of English at the University of Nebraska – Lincoln, explains that Whitman had relocated for a few months to Boston to oversee the printing and production of the third edition of *Leaves of Grass*.[6] Along with being publishers, Thayer and Eldridge were abolitionists and financial supporters of John Brown. It appears, says Price, that the publishing office at 1116 Washington Street was a gathering place for like-minded folks. Price adds that Silas also met Universalist Unitarian Rev. Thomas Wentworth, who had also been a John Brown financial supporter. He was also one of the "Secret Six," a group of five other New England and New York abolitionists who supported John Brown and his cause to dismantle the system of enslavement.[7]

Silas begins this letter with an overview of his amazing travels from Boston to Lawrence, traveling on every possible 19th century mode of transportation to get home. The details of this trip illustrate his sense of humor, as he writes about the delays of travel, and includes an invitation to Walt to come to Lawrence, "and when he comes out here the folks will treat him well."

---

6. Email from Dr. Kenneth Price to author, August 13, 2024.
7. *John Brown and the Secret Six*, Massachusetts Historical Society, accessed December 20, 2024, https://www.masshist.org/features/boston-abolitionists/john-brown.

The letter shifts to announce that he is going to Pikes Peak with his brother and cousin to join the many other Fifty Niners who crossed the plains to the new Queen City of Denver in search of gold, dragging along a quartz machine. David Forsyth, executive director and curator at the Gilpin County Historical Society, says that quartz machine was also known as a stamp mill, and was used for crushing ore, or rock, in search for gold veins.[8] Note dear reader, that I am not using the word "pioneer." The word pioneer intimates that the those who came to the Colorado Territory following the 1859 gold rush, were the first to be on this land, and that is not so. Indigenous people traveled the land for centuries. I am attempting to decenter whiteness in the storytelling of this book by not using "pioneer."

And then Silas describes an event to Thayer, Eldridge and Hinton that has just happened with a person named Stewart, who was escorting formerly enslaved people, when a young free Black boy has been stolen in a kidnapping that he has witnessed. Take note, he identifies some of the people present with only an initial, or last name, I suspect so they can't be identified, but clearly everyone is in the know of who they are, especially the Boston abolitionists. Read the letter, again. Note that the event reveals a sub-text, that Silas is explaining about who is present at this kidnapping, and who goes after the child. I think "Stewart" in this letter is Captain James L. Stewart, one of The Immortal 10 (see timeline), and who lived southeast of Lawrence on a farm that was considered one of the busiest Underground Railroad stations in Kansas Territory. "By the spring of 1860, slave catchers from Missouri were more emboldened than ever and raided his farm, capturing one young lad whom they took back to St. Joseph," writes Todd Mildfelt.[9] I suspect that this may be the very same event that Silas witnesses and writes about in this letter.

---

8. David Forsyth, interview with author, Central City, CO, November 12, 1864.

9. Todd Mildfelt, "The Underground Railroad in Kansas," Symphony in

After consulting with Byron Strom, family letter expert, we suspect that the references are to Kansans whom Thayer, Eldridge, and maybe Hinton, all met in Harrisburg or Boston, recruited to come east by Hinton.[10] The Kansans who were there included James Montgomery and four others, including Silas who were part of The Immortal Ten, S.J. Willis, Joseph Gardner and Joshua A. Pike. The other Kansans were Carpenter, Seamans, and Rice, using only last names to identify them. One may be able to conclude that Thayer, Eldridge and Hinton know who these men are, but maybe G is Joseph Gardner, M is for James Montgomery, and S is for Seamans? Could "Stearns" be George L. Stearns, one of the "Secret Six" who financially supported John Brown for his Harpers Ferry Raid?[11]

Give my love to all, he writes at the end of this first letter. He is a man who has big feelings and is not at all shy in expressing them to these men whom he clearly loves. Fellow abolitionists. Fellow friends who have put themselves in harm's way doing what they think is right. We see a circle of men in this letter who he is in community with doing acts of justice, caring for those who are seeking freedom out of enslavement and the selling of human beings. This is not the only letter where he writes, "give my love to all," but this is the first. What would the world look like if we shared that expression with fellow justice seekers?

Unbeknownst in May when he writes this letter that by the fall of 1860, his father, Amasa dies in Lawrence. His obituary speaks of a husband and father who was the "apostle of Liberty." It documents his journey from his birthplace of Woolwich, ME to Bath where he was a cooper, one who made

---

the Flint Hills Field Journal New Prairie Press, Kansas State University Libraries, 2011, 58, accessed December 20, 2024, https://newprairiepress.org/sfh/2011/flinthills/6/, 58.
10. Byron Strom, phone interview with author, December 9, 2024.
11. Reynolds, *John Brown, Abolitionist*, 211.

and repaired wooden barrels and casks, and then to Chelsea, MA, where he lived until "at the call of duty, he girded up his loins, buckled on his armor and started for Kansas, emulating his forefathers... They make the West, as they the East, The homestead of the free." The obituary continues to explain that the cause of death stemmed from "the exposures, hardships, and disease incident to pioneer life seemed too much for his constitution, and for several years much ill health has fallen to his lot, until, on the evening of Friday the 28th of September yielding to exhaustion consequent upon cholera morbus, he breathed his last."[12]

Silas never writes about the death of his father. We don't know if he traveled back to Lawrence to be with his mother and siblings. As this year ends and a New Year begins, he writes next in July 1861 from the Colorado Territory as a blacksmith in Missourie City, making just enough money for food, and by the end of the year, enlists in Black Hawk as a Union soldier in the American Civil War.

---

12. Obtained from *The Republican* published October 4, 1860, in Lawrence, KS. Collected from the Kansas State Historical Society files by Malcolm Strom, courtesy of Byron Strom.

Chapter Three
The Letter, 1861 – A Mining Life

When the Confederate artillery blasted Fort Sumter and launched the American Civil War on April 18, 1861, the nation was sliced open into two. The original transcription of this letter that I first saw 15 years ago listed Missourie City, in Kansas Territory, but in fact, Silas writes from Missourie City, Colorado Territory. Colorado Territory was founded on February 28, 1861, and this letter was written just four months later. Missourie City was located south of Central City, Colorado Territory and was a bustling town of tents when Silas was there. It is now a ghost town, marked only by the grave of a child, Clara Delaney, on a parkway heading from Central City to I-70.

Letter Three
to Major James B. Abbott

July 21st, 1861
Lawrence, Kansas

Old Friend,

I can't hear anything reliable from you so I think the best thing I can do is to write. I hear that you are Agent for the Shawnees. I am very glad to hear of that. It will suit you and I suppose it will pay. You may thank your stars Major that you left this country when you did for it is deader than it ever was and has been ever since you left. We expected a large emigration here this spring but it has been very small and what has come have gone to the southern mines and from there back home or else to California or some other foreign country. The fact is Major I am getting D--n sick of this God forsaken place. There are very few Lodes paying and but few mills running. I am still at work in the shop. I have carried it on myself for the last three months and have got so that I am quite a smith.

Warden and some of the Boys have been prospecting over the range but have found nothing. What is the show back there? Could I get a Lieutenant's commission in the army or anything of the kind? If I could I would go back. If not I shall stick to the shop until fall and then put out for Carson Valley, Washoe or California or else I will go to South America or some other outlandish place. Bill Roe and wife and George Roe have gone to California. They started two weeks ago. Jack Gill is in Delaware Gulch over the range. I guess he is not doing much. Dick Erwin started over in that direction. George Cutter has the only team on this gulch and is doing the best of any one hauling. Frank [Varnum] is working in gold run.

He has bought [a] part of a claim there. He makes grub and not much more. Boynton worked out my claim. He took out $400. We get 1/4 of it which is fifty dollars apiece. George got his and I am waiting for mine to send back to Bill. I have been expecting to hear from you in regard to the things you left here. I don't know how Harsh and Stearns have done. I bought a pair of boots of Stearns and told him I would pay for them before you came out. I haven't paid for them yet. I got a pair on the same terms on an order of

Boyntons at Harshes. Your things at Boyntons I expect she has ransacked as I have noticed any quantity of cigars laying about. She furnishes Dr. Harsh with all he can smoke. She says the mice has eat them most all up. I got some there last week and I was up today looking at them and took five or six. The mice have been in them but I don't think they have done much damage. Any business I can do for you I will tend to if you will let me know. I want to pay you what I owe you as soon as I can, but I have not made much more than grub since you left but I will pay you all I owe you before I leave the country. I believe I owe you more than anybody else. Will I pay Stearns and Boynton for their boots or pay it to you?

I wish you would let me take that snuff box at Boyntons. I will take good care of it and return it when and where you want it. I want it for fine cut chewing tobacco. I am glad to hear that JL has the appointment of Brigadier General but am sorry he lost his seat in the senate by it. I think the Coal Creek Boys ought to be whipped for giving up the cannon. If us boys go back this fall I think we will have it if it is in the country or break something. Mrs. Raff is in good spirits. She often inquires about you. Write as soon as you can. Give me all the news. What is the chance of getting a Deputy under you? Is there nothing I can do that will pay? Any business I can do for you here I will tend to up to the handle. Do you ever see Bill? If you do tell him that Stearns wants him to let Wilmarth have his revolver. I forgot to write him about it in my last. Stearns is doing well in his book store. I don't think of any more that would interest you. Answer soon and direct to Missourie[sic] City.

                                        Yours &c.
                                        Sile

[in the margin] I expect you will have hard work to read this but I am in a hurry. This is not my best.

-Anne E. Hemphill Collection

***

There are lots of boys from Coal Creek, Kansas Territory in Gilpin County mining for gold, and Silas references many of them in this letter to James B. Abbott. The ghost town of Missourie City is south of today's Central City, a historical town that is one of three gambling communities in Colorado. Black Hawk is east of Central City, and between Central City and Black Hawk is the ghost town of Mountain City. All of these were bustling mining towns of tents when Silas wrote this letter.

James B. Abbott is indeed an old friend of the Soule family. And by old friend, the Soule family and James B. Abbott go back most likely to 1854 when James and Amasa Soule arrived in Lawrence within a month of each other. James is one of The Immortal 10, as is Silas, who went to Missouri to break out Dr. John Doy from a St. Joseph prison after he was arrested for traveling with formerly enslaved people seeking freedom in the Kansas Territory. In a 1929 interview with *The Kansas City Star*, Silas' sister, Annie, recalled the story of The Immortal 10. "The exploit has been called the most daring and chivalrous of all the deeds of free-state men. Doy was guiding sixteen escaped slaves, three of them women and two children, to a station on the Underground railway [Railroad] at Holton, when twenty mounted and armed men from Missouri captured the whole company and took them to Weston, Mo. The sixteen Negroes were sold back into slavery and Doy was tried in St. Joseph for abducting slaves, was convicted and sentenced to five years in the penitentiary.

"Ten men of Lawrence and vicinity, under James B. Abbott, went to St. Joseph. My brother went into the jail first and reconnoitered and that night the party bound one of their number, pretended he was a horse-thief and said they wanted to lodge him in jail for safekeeping until morning. By this ruse they got into the jail, held up the jailer and took Doy out and across the river into Kansas."[1] When I first visited the Kansas State Historical Society in Topeka, KS in 2008 doing research on Silas, a huge photo of The Immortal 10 hung in the first floor lobby of the museum, a testimony if you will of the commitment of free staters to keep Kansas free.

Silas and James, who was 20 years Silas' senior, were cut from the same cloth in the large abolition, free-staters community in Kansas. There is no evidence that they knew each other in New England, but it would not be surprising, especially knowing their strong commitment to leave their homes to help keep Kansas free.

An 1859 guide book for miners coming to Pike's Peak to "reap a golden reward,' writes to young miners like Silas with a heavy dose of hope.[2] "...the young man, whose hands are free – who has a strong constitution and stronger moral courage; who has no permanent paying business in the States – let such go and with industry and perseverance he may reap a golden reward.

"All will not be equally successful – some are doomed to disappointment. Therefore, let each make up his mind to be content with a moderate gain, as a result of persevering toil and severe hardships, and if by chance he should be among the most successful, the pleasurable emotions experienced

---

1. A.B. MacDonald, "She Looks Back Seventy-Five Years to the Founding of Lawrence," *Kansas City Star*, January 13, 1929, 1.
2. "The Illustrated Miners' Hand-book and Guide to Pike's Peak with a New and Reliable Map, Showing all the Routes, and the Gold Regions of Western Kansas and Nebraska," (Saint Louis, MO: Parker & Huyett, 1859), 29.

will be proportionably greater." Few really ever had success, but all had big expectations of making a fortune.

Silas seems to be one of those young miners who was doomed to disappointment and with this letter, appears to have reached his max of Missourie City. Somewhat bored and disillusioned in the day-to-day work of mining and now blacksmithing, he reaches out to Abbott asking what the possibilities are of coming home. He hopes for better, and really as we will see in future letters, longs to get back to Lawrence. Could this be a way, he asks? Remember, reader that the Civil War erupted in April of this year. Union men are being recruited to serve throughout the Northern states, so his hope that there is a possible lieutenant's commission is a way out and a way home. But he is so endearing about other possibilities, he's thinking of California or South America, or "some other outlandish place" to land.

Clearly, Abbott has been to the Colorado Territory, and specifically to Missourie City, though I found nothing in my research of such a trip. I love reading the details of how men in mining camps are trying to make do, on credit, on trade, and occasionally on barter. It was very hard work. We know from his next letter that he didn't stay a miner in Gilpin County for long, but this letter illustrates the many hardships, especially the financial that he is experiencing. As this letter shows, he is quite connected with the Coal Creek-Lawrence men he came with a year earlier. Reader, did you notice that old friend George Cutter is in Missourie City with Silas? According to Davd Forsyth, at the Gilpin County Historical Society, George is "hauling ore" to be taken to Black Hawk, where Silas will enlist in the American Civil War in just a few months. It was the "city of mills," said Forsyth, because the land was flatter, and more water was available.[3]

---

3. David Forsyth, Interview with author, Central City, CO, November 12, 2024.

And Bill? Bill is his brother, William Lloyd Garrison, named after the Boston abolitionist and publisher of the abolitionist Boston newspaper, *The Liberator*. Silas inquires about Bill in many of these letters, but there is not a letter to Bill in the collection. He writes occasionally as we will see, but Bill didn't save Silas' letters. The reason we have this magnificent collection of family letters is because Silas' mom, and two sisters, Em and Annie, someday after his death, I suspect, put this collection of letters literally together, each one donating to the greater whole to the collection.

Silas most likely refers to "J" in this letter as being appointed brigadier general as James Henry Lane, who was appointed in June 1861 as brigadier general of Kansas volunteers by President Abraham Lincoln. In that same 1929 interview, Annie mentioned that she knew "Jim Lane" ... "very well indeed." She mentions that "he had been to our house and I have heard him speak many times."[4]

Sam Bock, director of interpretation and publications at History Colorado, said that by the time Silas wrote this letter the Territory already was in its second wave of gold miners, a more realistic bunch, than the first wave who followed the trail to the Territory after hearing from boosters that gold was so prolific that one could find gold nuggets on the ground just for the looking. "They were more realistic."[5] Bock described places like Gold Hill and Missourie City as towns that would look like tent cities in 1861. "All these guys have made claims or are mining in streams," said Bock. The mills that Silas refers to are the processing sites that are processing the gold out of the ore, or the rock. Miners would be paid by the mills either by buying the gold, or by giving the gold to the miner, with a processing fee. These boom or bust places were simply a collection of tents, but the most important tent was the saloon, where miners would pay for drinks

---

4. MacDonald, 1.
5. Sam Bock, phone interview with author, October 11, 2024.

with gold dust. These mining towns were "instant cities," said Bock. He explained that "grub" which Silas writes about is food, or vittles. The "worked out my claim" is that he was digging or doing the work of a miner. Bock describes the share that Silas writes about as a communal share, that all the men he refers to pooled their resources together in hope that a vein of gold would be found. Veins could run for miles, but whoever gets to mine the vein depends on the locations of the veins. Pooling resources, having a communal share all would help address the number one problem of looking for gold, labor, said Bock. On a side note, Bock noted that this letter simply sounds like a description of everyday life for Silas, and "it looks like he knows everyone in town," adding that the business conducting he writes about, sounds like today's emails."

Today, the grave of child Clara Delaney sits alongside the new parkway just outside of Central City, leading to I-70, and marks the only spot where the town of tents of Missourie City was originally located. Her gravestone, originally marble, has long gone, and in its place a wood marker, surrounded by a large metal fence, makes known a once bustling mining town that has long ago faded away. Workers at the town of Central City installed this magnificent fence and now maintain her grave. At the end of 1861, a year of mining, blacksmithing, and meeting up with other Lawrence men in Gilpin County, Silas enlists in the United States Army on December 11 in Black Hawk, and begins 1862 writing his first letter to poet Walt Whitman in the first few days of the new year.

Chapter Four
The Letters, 1862 – War, Hope and Family

Silas enlisted in the US Army in Black Hawk, Colorado Territory in December 1861. He gave the return address in this first letter to Walt Whitman as Camp Weld, which was a 30-acre military encampment, built in 1861 near Denver, in what is now the La Alma-Lincoln Park neighborhood. A plaque on a neighborhood building at 2045 Vallejo St. is the only indicator of the existence of this historic 19th century camp that housed hundreds of men in 1862. The postmark of Mountain City, Colorado Territory is indeed in the mountains, population was 800 when Silas wrote this letter to Walt. In the winter of 1862, where "the wind blows a perfect hurricane, and it is cold as Greenland," he sounds warm and content. If only we knew what Walt wrote back! Silas wrote many more letters this year than in 1861 in our collection. Mining life might have kept him away from writing letters, as well as discerning about his enlistment in the American Civil War.

Letter Four
to Walt Whitman

January 8th, 1862
Rocky Mountains

Friend Walt

Perhaps you have forgotten a wild harum scareum young man who used to linger around Thayer and Eldridge Publishing's office, Boston, in the spring of 1860. But he still remembers you and has been waiting very patiently for a volume of Leaves of Grass which was to be sent to Lawrence, Kansas. Perhaps you think I am writing very familiar for almost a stranger and writing to a distinguished Poet but I think I have made a sufficient apology when I tell you I have been in the Rocky Mountains for almost two years where every man is an old acquaintance if you never saw him before. When I left Boston I came to Kansas and from there out here among Grizzly bears, Indians, yankees and almost every species of man and beast that inhabits the globe. I have lived on venison and I have lived on bread. I have gone hungry for many a day and have had plenty to eat for many more. And for all the hard ships I have seen, it suits me. I like it. I enjoy myself hugely, and I think you would do the same.

I now hold the position of 1st Lieut. of Co. K, 1st Reg Col Vols and suppose I shall be a soldier for the next few years.

I have often heard <u>Leaves of Grass</u> highly spoken of away out here but have never seen a volume until a few days ago and the man who has that will not dispose of that for any [thing]. He brought it out with him to this country.

I am in an old log shanty tonight up in the mountains about forty miles from the valley. The wind blows a perfect hurracane [sic] and it is cold as Greenland. I am writing by the light of a pitch pine fire. It is past twelve o'clock and I must go to bed as I must [head] for the valley in the morning. I don't want you to forget to answer this.

Good night
Yours &c Silas S. Soule

Please direct
Lieut S.S. Soule
Camp Weld, Denver, Col Ter.

[Envelope is addressed: Walt Whitman, Brooklyn, New York]

[Postmark: Mountain City, Colorado Territory, January 13, [18]62]

-Charles Feinberg Collection
Walt Whitman Archives
Library of Congress

***

There is such an air of familiarity in this letter for two men who have not seen each other in almost two years. Silas hopes to refresh Walt's memory by describing who he was in Boston, still longs for a copy of *Leaves of Grass*, and offers yet another invitation to Walt to come West.

This familiarity captures my heart in this letter. Silas sounds at peace, despite being at war, and with the mystery of the unknown of what is around the corner. This quote, "I have lived on venison and I have lived on bread. I have gone hungry for many a day and have had plenty to eat for many more. And for all the hardships I have seen, it suits me. I like it. I enjoy myself hugely," expresses a man who despite seeing hardships, finds himself telling Walt Whitman, that all is well.

We don't see this sense of peace in any other letter. This intimate language between men that Silas offers up in this letter, also captures my heart. Whitman, Thayer, Eldridge, Hinton, and Abbott, are part of this group of men, of abolitionists in solidarity with each other and a cause, and for the most part under the radar with their commitment to justice for transporting formerly enslaved people on the Underground Railroad. They are also some of the men who had been financially supporting John Brown. This is not a large circle of men, but they are close. They must have been able to count on each other in harrowing and extreme circumstances, and their trust has been earned.

I find this enduring "good night" sign off as another clue to how Silas expresses big feelings. He does not sign off any other letter in this collection with the expression of "good night." I'm moved by this endearing expression of gentleness to a friend.

He is at Camp Weld, newly constructed in September 1861, as a response to the outbreak of the American Civil War. According to his military records, Silas is at Camp Weld all month in January.

I have no evidence that he ever received a copy of *Leaves of Grass*.

His enthusiasm for being a soldier is clear, and imagines soldiering for the next few years, and honestly one would expect this kind of enthusiasm for someone who had just enlisted a month earlier and has not experienced any fighting. We shall read in his next letter to Walt, written from Fort Union, NM, that soldiering has become "rather rough." He has just marched with a regiment of men 400 miles in 15 days, and nothing is quite the same.

A note about Charles Feinberg, who donated these three letters to the Library of Congress, and the Walt Whitman Collection. It appears that Feinberg was a collector of all things Walt Whitman. How he came to start collecting ephemera of Walt's is a bit of a mystery, but his collection at the Library of Congress is quite vast. And on a side note, Walt himself saved both letter and envelope of Silas' correspondence. Together, they tell a story of letter writing and letter keeping.

***

Letter Five
to Walt Whitman

March 12th, 1862
Fort Union, New Mexico

Friend Walt,

I was very glad to get a letter from you and should have answered it before this but I had to march for New Mexico. Col Canby, who has command of the Union troops in NM has had a terrible encounter with Sibley of the Texas Rangers. Canby had only eight hundred white men and one Reg[iment] of Mexicans under the renowned Kit Carson. Sibley had three thousand men. Our white men done all the fighting, for the Mexicans broke and ran at the first fire. Our men fought like tigers. One company of Pikes Peak Boys was cut to pieces. Only seventeen survived the fight. The[y] emptied thirtyfive Texan saddles the first fire. Our loss of killed and wounded was about 225, the Texans about 400. As soon as we heard of the battle we made a forced march to the rescue. We marched a Reg[iment] of men 350 miles in 14 days. We marched 120 miles in three days and 80 miles in 24 hours. I think we made the biggest march on record. We understood that

Sibley was making an attact [sic] on Fort Union. The word came to us about sundown after the men had marched 40 miles and had not had their supper and they threw their hats in the air and swore they would march 40 miles farther before they slept and they did. They started off singing the Star spangled banner, Red white and Blue, and yankee doodle, so you can imagine what kind of material this Reg is composed of. We are now at Ft. Union without a fight but start in three days to attact [sic] Sibley where I expect we shall have as great a battle as ever was known.

Soldiering suits me although it is rather rough at present. We have traveled through mountains and plains and seen many amusing things. We have a splendid chance to study human nature for we have all kinds of men in the Reg. We are within one hundred miles of Santa Fee [sic] which I suppose is taken by the Texans by this time. Men, women, and children and thousands of head of stock arrive here daily from that country. They are all glad to see the soldiers. Thre[e] or four companies of the 5th infantry Regulars will march with us. We go direct to Santa Fee. I am afraid this letter will not be very interesting for I don't feel like writing. Direct to Lieut. S.S. Soule, 1st Reg Col Vols, Santa Fee, New Mexico.

Yours.
S.S. Soule

[Envelope is addressed to Walt Whitman, Brooklyn, New York]

-Charles Feinberg Collection
Walt Whitman Archives
Library of Congress

***

In this letter, Silas writes to Walt in the aftermath of the Battle of Valverde in New Mexico, the first of the three New Mexico engagements in the American Civil War. He is at Fort Union, which is today near Watrous, NM and an exit off of the I-25 highway. This is the only letter that he writes about an experience, in this case the Battle at Valverede, that he was not there to witness any of it.

In 1862, Silas would have stayed in the second Fort Union, built as an escarpment just a few months before his arrival. It is carved out of the land, and in this type of construction it looked like a five-point star. One really must look long and hard for any evidence of the second fort at Fort Union, which is now overgrown by grass. At the time Silas was at Fort Union, it was a bustling stop on the busy Santa Fe Trail, a beacon for travelers and traders alike, on their way to Santa Fe, or heading back to Franklin, MO. Today, you can see what is left of the third Fort Union, built out of wood, brick, adobe, by local craftsmen instead of soldiers, said Park Ranger Trinidad Gallegos (Hispanic-white), who has worked at Fort Union for 16 years.[1] His family has lived for generations in the area, and two of his ancestors, Trinidad Lopez and Santiago Bonnie, served at Fort Union in the 19th century. Our three-hour walkabout took us through the relics of commissaries, barracks, and the parade ground, where a 120-feet flagpole and flag flying would have been a landmark for Santa Fe travelers who upon seeing the flag, would have known they were very close. If you're fortunate enough when you visit, you can see local craftsmen doing preservation work on adobe to help keep what is left still standing. I was fortunate to chat with Preservationist Jaime Salazar, who lives close by and has

---

1. Trinidad Gallegos, interview with author, Watrous, NM, September 24, 2024.

been making and applying adobe to the existing walls of Fort Union for nine years.

This letter begins with a detailed description of the Battle of Valverde, near Fort Craig, south of Albuquerque on February 21, 1862. Silas writes in intimate detail to Walt, as if he was there, but he wasn't. When I met with historian John Taylor, and author of *Bloody Valverde, A Civil War Battle on the Rio Grande,* February 21, 1862, at the Isleta Casino, located on the Isleta Reservation south of Albuquerque, he immediately knew that Silas was passing along information that he had most likely gleaned from sitting with others around the campfire at Fort Union and passing along inaccurate information.[2] He refers "to 'our white men did all the fighting and the Mexicans broke and ran at the first fire,' which is not at all what happened," says Taylor.

It had been a long day in battle, explained Taylor, "with Union soldiers crossing the Rio Grande, and Confederates mustering a defense with artillery shells which most Union soldiers had never seen."[3] The "Mexicans" whom Silas refers to in this letter are the men of the 2nd Regiment New Mexico Volunteers under command of Colonel Miguel Pino. Taylor writes in his book, "that Colonel Canby ordered the 2nd Regiment of New Mexico Volunteers forward to a position about eight hundred yards from the Confederate's ridgeline position, to draw the Texan's fire so that their deployment, particularly their battery locations, could be confirmed. Suddenly, with the strains of a brass band drifting overhead, a series of explosions shattered the late afternoon shadows."[4] With that, Pino's men retreated and deserted. Not after first fire, as Silas suggests, but after being confronted with the work-

---

2. John Taylor, interview with author, Albuquerque, NM, September 22, 2024.
3. John Taylor, phone interview with author, December 5, 2024.
4. John Taylor, *Bloody Valverde, A Civil War Battle on the Rio Grande, February 21, 1862,* (Albuquerque, NM: University of New Mexico, Albuquerque, 1995), 36.

ing end of a Confederate cannon after a long, first-time day of battle.[5] No one ever knows what will happen in a battle, but the rumor that the 2nd Regiment New Mexico Volunteers ran at first fire is simply not true. Silas wasn't there to pass this telephone game on to Walt Whitman, so how did he hear the news of the Battle of Valverde? When he gets to Fort Union where he writes this letter, none of the soldiers there were at the battle. The Colorado Volunteers who were there, stayed at Fort Craig, so they didn't share the news-rumor account. It's possible that whoever shared the news of the Battle of Valverde to spurn on the Great March to Fort Union from Camp Weld might have shared this with Silas, but the details in this letter are not the kind of details that would have been shared. All that needed to be shared to get the soldiers on the Great March would be 'Confederates are in New Mexico. Come quickly.' It's a mystery by all accounts, but whoever passed along the inaccurate story, around the campfire, or on the Great March, passed along the language of "whites" and "Mexicans," and it speaks of racial overtones, said Taylor. Or of racism in the ranks.

The Great March from Camp Weld to Fort Union, is most likely "the biggest march in record," Silas writes to Walt. Just imagine the challenges of feeding and watering soldiers and horses alike, for this amazing feat of marching 400 miles in 15 days. While the landscape is mostly flat, the army traveled over Raton Pass at an elevation of 7,835. The weather in February could have been anything from robin egg blue sky to a horrific snowstorm.

On my pilgrimage to New Mexico to see where Silas had been, and to see what he saw if I could, I traveled to Fort Craig and the battlefield at Valverde, then north to the town and battlefield of Peralta. Then onto Santa Fe where I visited the grave of his beloved friend Major Edward Wynkoop who is buried at the National Military Cemetery. While in Santa Fe,

---

5. Taylor, *Bloody Valverde*, 37.

I meandered a bit (cause pilgrimages are made to do some meandering!), exploring and having several greats meal at LaFonda, one of the oldest hotels just off the historic plaza, which Silas would have seen. He would have also seen the Palace of the Governors after he traveled the Santa Fe Trail to Santa Fe, a town where Samuel and Susan Shelby Magoffin visited and she wrote about in her diary in 1846, sixteen years before Silas showed up and saw the same historic plaza that she did.[6] Then I headed north to the Battle of Glorieta Pass – Pecos National Historical Park in Pecos, NM, and then north to Fort Union, where this letter was written.

A monument in the Santa Fe Plaza, now tells the story of the toppling of a war monument at the historic plaza, built originally to honor the soldiers who fought at the three battles of the New Mexico Campaign in the American Civil War. Following the murder of George Floyd in 2020, the national protest landed on the steps of this historic plaza, with protestors taking down the obelisk on the war monument. Over the years since its installation, the monument panels had been revised, to include a panel that read "to the heroes who have fallen in the various battles with the savage Indians of the Territory of New Mexico," until 1974 when the word savage was chiseled off.[7] The city of Santa Fe had received complaints about the language for decades. Along with the obelisk that was toppled, the panels of the monument have been covered over with plywood. Today, a sign at the monument includes language about a "Resolution Hosting Community Conversations on Santa Fe's Cultures, Histories, Art, Reconciliation and Truth," and that the "City's Leadership recognizes

---

6. Photo of Magoffin-Fishe Home Site (La Fonda Parking Garage), El Camino Real de Tierra Adentro Historic Trail, Old Spanish National Historic Trail, Santa Fe National Historic Trail, National Park Service, December 6, 2024.

7. John C. Bienvenu, "Making Sense of Santa Fe's Soldiers' Monument: Part One," August 25, 20022, accessed December 20, 2024, https://bienvenulaw.com/2022/08/25/making-sense-of-santa-fes-soldiers-monument/.

the need to create a process for community engagement to encourage people to speak, to be heard, and to listen."[8]

The Union soldier that was part of the Civil War monument at the State Capitol in Denver, also was toppled during the George Floyd national protest in 2020. While Gov. Jared Polis was "outraged" at the damage to the statue that commemorates Colorado soldiers who fought and lost their lives in the American Civil War (including the Sand Creek Massacre), and promised that "this statue will be repaired and we will use every tool at our disposal to work with the Denver Police and to hold accountable those responsible for the damage whether they are hooligans, white supremacists, Confederate sympathizers, or drunk teenagers."[9] This monument named the officers at the Sand Creek Massacre, and Silas' name was there.[10] If there is a future for this monument restoration in conversation with the community, it is not being discussed publicly.

All this to be said, place is powerful in our past and in our present. It can provide a sense of comfort to return to something familiar or connectional, whether it be of a biological ancestor, or in my case, an ancestor of choice, which is how I sometimes like to describe Silas. If we can choose a family of choice, we most certainly can choose an ancestor of choice.

---

8. Photo of signage, September 18, 2024.
9. John Frank and Evan Oshsner, "Civil War monument at Colorado Capitol town down and marred by graffiti," *The Colorado Sun*, June 25, 2020, https://coloradosun.com/2020/06/25/civil-war-monument-colorado-capitol/.
10. In the final days of editing, the design of a new monument at the former Civil War Monument that was toppled, was announced in April 2025. The design was approved by the Colorado Legislature and is expected to be a 24-foot-tall sculpture of an Arapaho chief, a Cheyenne chief and an Indigenous woman holding a child. Colorado Public Radio also reported that it will be installed in 2026. "Sand Creek Massacre memorial to replace Civil War Statue at the Colorado State Capitol," Colorado Public Radio, by Lucas Brady Woods, KUNC accessed on May 8, 2025, https://www.cpr.org/2025/04/15/sand-creek-massacre-memorial-to-replace-civil-war-statue-at-the-colorado-state-capitol/

When I walked the well-preserved parade ground at Fort Garland, I knew Silas had walked this same parade ground. For me, it was just one of the sacred and holy moments of connection to him and the past. In the midst of hearing 21st century traffic along the highway close by, I was reminded that he was here. As I'm writing this, I'm reminded that this was one of those pilgrimage moments that can still create a lump in my throat. Eleanor Haley writes about nostalgia, which this may very well be, in the longing for or returning to a place, especially in grief. She writes, "Johannes Hofer first described nostalgia back in 1688. The word he chose, 'nostalgia,' breaks down into the Greek words 'notos,' which means homecoming and 'algos,' which means pain. His observations were based on Swiss mercenaries in France and Italy whose nostalgia for their home country was so intense he theorized that they had a neurological disorder. Later, similar observations were made by physicians working in the French Revolutionary Army and the American Civil War."[11] Haley calls it a coping mechanism. I simply call it comforting to return to a place of connection with Silas close by, separated by 160 years of history. But I also feel nostalgic visiting my hometown of Flagstaff, AZ, or a childhood favorite pizzeria in Tenafly, NJ, of my mom's favorite bakery near Harstein Island, WA. I'm affirming for you, and for me, that place is powerful and returning to it can be healing, helpful, and maybe a homecoming with pain, as well.

Silas writes he will go direct to Santa Fe, but within two weeks from writing this letter, he will find himself on the land where the Pecos Pueblo had lived for centuries at the Battle of Glorieta Pass in his first battle with the Confederates, under the command of Major John Chivington.

***

---

11. Eleanor Haley, "Understanding Nostalgia in Grief: A Deep Dive," What's Your Grief, whatsyourgrief.com, accessed on April 6, 2025.

Letter Six
to Walt Whitman

Undated
[May-June 1862]
Camp Valverdi, near Fort Craig, New Mexico

Friend Walt,

I received a letter from you last March and answered it while at Ft. Union but have never heard from you since. Well, here I am camped on a sand bank on the Rio Grande River. The weather is hot and we have very little of the good things of America in the shape of Grub and Clothing but we have a regament [sic] composed of nature's Nobleman. We left Denver pourly [sic] clothed and equipped. In the month of February [we] marched to Fort Union, a distance of four hundred miles in fifteen days. Two days we marched forty miles a day and then hearing that the Texans were marching on Fort Union we marched over seventy miles in twenty four hours. I believe that was the best marching made by any Reg in the service. We being short of provisions and destitute of Clothing, our men stood it bravely and never murmured.

The Texans, flushed with success, having whipped three thousand Regular and volunteer mexican [sic] troops at Fort Craig were marching boldly on towards Fort Union laying the country waste wherever they went. We, all eager to try our Reg marched one hundred miles and met the enemy on their own ground in Apache Canon [sic] in the mountains, our force of nine hundred, theirs of two thousand.[12] We fought seven hours, sometimes hand to hand over rocks, stumps and trees, regular bush whacking Indian fighting. The Texans' loss was about five hundred killed and wounded, ours about one hundred and eighty. We burned sixty of their wagons loaded with provisions, clothing, ammunition and valuables, leaving them destitute. They commenced their retreat the next day we followed a few days afts joined Gen. Canby's force at Alberquerque [sic], drove the enemy two hundred miles like a flock of sheep. At Peralto we had another little battle where we took seven wagons and a number of Prisoners. They said they did not mind fighting Regular troops, but there was no use fighting Chivington's Grey blouse Pikes Peak Sons of bitches so they burned all they had and fled to the mountains making for Texas with all possible speed, and I am inclined to believe that they will never have any inclination to come to New Mexico again.

Our Colonel Chivington was a methodist Preacher, "Presiding" elder in Colorado. He is about six feet four inches high and built in proportion, a first rate fellow and liked by his Regament [sic]. We have marching orders now to join Col Carlton's California troops about three hundred miles south of here. I expect we will start in about a week. We are getting tired of lying still although we have our sports. To night we have a swimming match for a purse of $30. They are to swim across the Rio Grande. Our boys have built houses for themselves, some of mud, some of willows and some have dug house[s] in the bank by the River and live quite comfortable. I am afraid you will not find much in this letter to interest you for I am in no humor for

---

12. A significant part of the Battle of Glorieta Pass occurred in Apache Canyon.

writing to day. I may do better next time. I hope to hear from you before long.

I remain your Friend
Lieut. Silas S. Soule
1st Reg Col Vols
<u>In the Field</u>

-Charles Feinberg Collection
Walt Whitman Archives
Library of Congress

***

While this letter is undated, Silas' company muster roll indicates that in March and April he was at Ft. Union. Historian John Taylor suspects this letter was written by Silas in either May or June 1862 as the weather is hot, but there is no information in his company muster roll that he was at Fort Craig. We can be sure it was written after the Battle of Peralta, April 18, which was fought south of Albuquerque and which he writes about in this letter. The Rio Grande travels differently today near Fort Craig than it did in 1862, and is much narrower, which can only help us to conclude that swimming competitions are a thing of the past.

After three battles in three months, the Confederates are on their way back to Texas and "I am inclined to believe that they will never have any inclination to come to New Mexico, again," which over time becomes true, Confederates don't return to New Mexico. On my pilgrimage to see the landscape he saw, and to connect to where he was, I came upon a lone Confederate monument just off the I-25 Highway at the San Marcial exit in isolated, rural central New Mexico located on more than 300,000 acres owned by Ted Turner.

In 1936, the Texas Division of the United Daughters of the Confederacy built and installed this monument in memory to the Texas Mounted Volunteers and all unknown soldiers killed in the Battle of Valverde. It can easily be missed, but it stands as a reminder that more than 70 years after the Confederates lost the American Civil War, this monument is a showcase that Confederates were here.

While he writes to Walt of his fighting, burning provisions, and often hand-to-hand combat, this is Silas' first engagement with an enemy in his military career. We will travel with him in the next two years as he grows into the military hierarchy and system of rank, becomes a captain and a recruiting officer, but this is the only time in his military career that he fights the Confederates, or fights anyone. He fought side-by-side with those who we will become very familiar with in Silas' letters in the next two years, Major Edward (Ned) Wynkoop, whom Silas will write a letter to with the horrific details of the Massacre at the peaceful camp of Cheyenne and Arapaho elders, women and children at Sand Creek, and Boston abolitionist Lt. Col. Samuel Tappan, who becomes the Fort Garland Post Commander, and then will be the president of the military commission at the Congressional Inquiry of the Sand Creek Massacre in 1865. These two men, who he went into battle with, will cross paths again and again in these letters as friends and colleagues.

His second battle with the Confederates was at Peralto where "we had another little battle where we took seven wagons and a number of Prisoners."

By the time Silas writes this letter about John Chivington with words of affection, terms of endearment, and as "a Methodist preaching, presiding elder in Colorado," Chivington has been promoted to Colonel following the win at the Battle of Glorieta Pass. We will read several letters in this collection in which Silas writes to Chivington from various places in the Colorado Territory on his travels. These terms of endearment will not last. All three, Silas, Ned, and Samuel, will express outrage, disgust, and speak truth to power after Sand Creek towards the Methodist preacher and presiding elder. Here, in the New Mexico Campaign of 1862, they find the trust in each other that being on a battlefield requires. If they weren't bonded already, the Battle of Glorieta Pass in March, where the men with Silas climbed down a ravine, watched Confederates die, lit wagons of supplies on fire, and climbed back up the ravine to rejoin the other regiments, tells the story of survival and trust.[13]

My pilgrimage to Fort Union, the battlefield at Glorieta Pass, and the battlefield of Peralta demonstrates the wide differences of how battlefields and forts are preserved in the American West today. At Peralta, which is now individually and privately owned, and is separated by a four-lane state road, there is a Catholic parish, a trailer park and overgrown landscape. If it wasn't for a highway sign marking the location, no one would know an American Civil War battle was fought there.

The battlefield at Valverde, which Silas was not at, but arrived maybe a month or two later, is adjacent to Fort Craig, where Silas writes this letter. It is now privately owned by Ted Turner. Fort Craig is owned by the Bureau of Land Management, which came late to the game of preserving and protecting the fort. No active preservation is happening, and there is very limited interpretation at Fort Craig today.

I meandered on two-lane roads, dirt roads, and a multi-lane highway to travel to these historic forts and battlefields. Silas would have been on his horse with soldiers, not always on a trail, but at times on the very worn, much-traveled Santa Fe Trail. Battlefield preservation looks very different in the American West than at other eastern American Civil War

---

13. Byron Parker, interview with author, Pecos, NM, September 23, 2024.

battlefields like Gettysburg, Manassas, Chickamauga, Shiloh and Antietam mostly because of encroaching development.

Individual ownership at Peralta and Valverde doesn't protect the landscape or preserve the property, like Fort Union and Glorieta does, in part because the latter are National Park Service properties. Peralta and Valverde battlefields also don't get the protection, preservation, and most importantly, interpretation of how these landscapes are connected in this New Mexico Campaign of 1862. There have been huge challenges in preserving these historic forts and battlefields, and those challenges will only become greater with limited resources and the ongoing aging properties, especially the fragile and tender adobe structures that are eroding back into the land.

This is the last letter Silas wrote to Walt.

Chapter Five
The Letters, 1863 – Denver

These family letters are connected to the horrific event in Lawrence on August 21, 1863, where pro-slavery Missourians raided Lawrence, destroying the town, and killing 150 men and boys.[1] The personal toll on the family was Mother's fear and Will's home, where $900 worth of books burned. Silas demonstrates many strong feelings in these letters, ranging from anger to compassion, to revenge and empathy.

Letter Seven
to his sister, Emily

September 4th, 1863
Denver, Colorado Territory

Dear Em,

I received your letter last night and was very glad to hear that you had all come out safe for I was very much afraid that Bill would go up the flume. I think you were all in luck. I am sorry that I have no money but I will

---

1. William Quantrill, accessed December 20, 2024, https://www.nps.gov/people/william-quantrill.htmnps.gov.

borrow $50.00 and send it. I want to go back there but don't see much chance now. I suppose Mother was scared some wasn't she? I hear that they have raised considerable money in Leavenworth for the sufferers.

I hope you will get some of it. I don't suppose you go much on Kansas now do you? I hope you will not go back for awhile. I shall try and get transferred to some Kansas Regiment. I want to get after some of those Missourians. We had the news here on the 23rd. It has caused some excitement for they were worse than Indians. I hope the Kansas Boys will desolate Missourie [sic] and not leave a house standing.

I sympathize with the sufferers at Lawrence and wish I was able to help them. Tell Mother to be brave and not fret over our loss. We will come out all right. Tell me in your next how much we lost there and where the house was-and all the particulars. I will write more next time. I have no time now as the mail will close soon.

Sile

[The following was written on the back of one of the pages of the letter.] If there is no one in Lawrence who knows the firm the within check is on, send it to Leavenworth or St. Joseph and they will cash it.

Sile

[On the back of the preceding letter, is a note from Annie J. Soule to her sister, Emily.]

Dear Em,

Will opened this letter and sent it to Mother with a note from himself. I got it for it was directed to Bath. Will had been sick with fever, but was better. You had better send this letter back after you have read it, for Mother will want to see it. Will didn't write anything new, said he missed things more than he had before. The folks were all well; he was going into the house the next week. His loss was more than he thought fore $900 by some of the books having been burned. He didn't mention Mary, nor anybody else except to say he had been helping Mac on his house. He doesn't expect any more troubles this year. Write as soon as you can. I didn't expect you to send me that money. Didn't you need it? I shall send Will's letter and the check to Mother for the check has to have her name and then be sent back to Kansas. Will says $2,000 wouldn't put him where he was before the fire. My love to Ella, tell her to write. Ask her "which she rather hab." No more in haste.

Annie

An additional note.

I unsealed the envelope to write that Mother expects to be here Saturday morning. What had I better get for a dress. I thought of getting one like yours but my whole extensive stock of dresses seems to be grey, just the color Mrs. Colman used to scold so about so I guess I'll try some other color. Write just as soon as you can.

Annie

-Anne E. Hemphill Collection

※※※

It has been more than a year since Silas left Denver in early 1862 on the Great March into New Mexico and he returned, writing to his sister Emily. As with many families in the 19th century, this letter, and response, circulated to other family members, who wrote additional notes, in this case, Silas' sister, Annie to Emily, and mailed it along to their mother. This is one way that families kept in touch through traveling letters with updates from other family members that were mailed and circulated for all to read.

The sweet way the Soule family added onto this letter makes it very interesting to dissect. It is the only letter in the collection where the family circulated a letter in this way. Of a significant historical note, the event Silas writes about in the first paragraph is the Lawrence Raid, also known as Quantrill's Raid on August 21. This raid, led by Confederate William Quantrill with 400 men, burned much of the town and killed 150 men and boys, possibly more who were never accounted for.

Firstly, here is another example of Silas' hope to get back to Kansas. We've already seen this desire come up in the letter with James Abbott, and we will see many more examples of his deepest desire to get home to Lawrence, or his ancestral home of Bath, ME.

Second, the "second" letter from Annie to her sister, Emily, describes the reality of some of Silas' fears at the Lawrence Raid had come true. Brother Will sustained significant damage in the Lawrence Raid with a fire and a considerable loss of books. This letter also indicates how well-traveled it has been, to Maine and back.

And lastly, Annie's sweet note at the end, that suggests she is getting a new dress, would have been a hoop dress, which was the style in the 1860s during the American Civil War. I'm not sure how I feel about her being "scolded" about the color grey, which seems to be all her dresses, but I do love that with this new dress, something will be different altogether.

The raid on Lawrence stemmed from ongoing conflicts between free staters in Kansas and those who were pro-enslavement in Missouri, just a stone's throw away from the border and Lawrence in 1863, now two years into the American Civil War. In January 1863 the Emancipation Proclamation was written by President Abraham Lincoln, declaring that enslaved people in southern states to be free, and authorizing the enlistment of Black troops. When Silas wrote this letter, the Battle of Gettysburg had happened just two months earlier. When we think about the Soule family traveling from New England in 1854, the potential for the Lawrence Raid, or something like it, might have been one of the reasons this family of abolitionists, and hundreds like them, came to Kansas in the 1850s.

The proximity to Missouri is also integral to rescuing Dr. John Doy from a St. Louis jail, after escorting formerly enslaved people to Kansas and freedom in 1859, only months before John Brown's raid at Harpers Ferry. We read in Silas' second letter, about witnessing an event where a formerly enslaved Black boy was recaptured on a Kansas farm south of Lawrence. Keeping Kansas free at all lengths, and costs, even from raids where deaths occurred and profound losses, was the commitment of abolitionists who put their lives at risk, that nothing else mattered but keeping Kansas free.

***

Letter Eight
to his sister, Annie

October 11th, 1863
Central City, Colorado Territory

Dear Annie,

I received a letter from you a day or two ago and was much surprised to ascertain that you were in Maine for I had not the least idea that you would go back, but I suppose you wanted take a visit anyhow. Do you think Mother and Em will ever go back to Kansas? I would like to see them when I get out of service. I wrote to Em as soon as I heard of the Lawrence raid and sent her $50. Did she get it? I hope so. I have not written a letter for so long that it is a task for me so I won't write much. Give my love to all the folks in Bath [Maine] and every where you may go. I am on recruiting service now, have been for two months. I like it well enough but it takes all my wages. I am Captain now and my pay is a little better than it was but I believe I will spend it as fast as I get it for fear it will get burned up if I try to save any.

This is not a very long letter, I only write to let you know I am all right.

Yours &c
Sile

-Anne E. Hemphill Collection

***

In 1863, it would take quite a few hours to travel from Golden, where he would pick up the Golden Gate Canyon Road and traverse over the front range of the Rocky Mountains to Central City. He's not far from Missourie City, or from Black Hawk where he enlisted in 1861, all located within five miles of each other. It seems he enjoyed getting away to a very familiar place. If he can't be home in Lawrence, I suspect Gilpin County is home away from home for Silas in the Colorado Territory.

Not a long letter, indeed! This letter to Annie is the shortest letter to a family member in the collection. The news of the day is that Silas announced his new rank of Captain, and with that comes a pay increase, but the role of recruiter, and the way he wants to re-enlist men in the Colorado Regiment becomes complicated in 1864, as we will see in his first letter of the new year.

I've been curious to know what kind of character or personality a soldier in 1863 needed to be good at the task of recruiting officer, so I asked some of the historians I interviewed for this book, what would it take? "He would have needed to be charismatic," said Park Ranger Trinidad Gallegos at Fort Union National Monument. "He also would have needed to convince people without trying," he added, noting he would have had to be "persistent."[2] On a visit to the Pecos National Historical Park, Park Ranger Byron Parker spread out maps to show exactly where Silas was at the Battle of Glorieta Pass, and specifically at Johnson's Ranch where they surprisingly came upon the Confederate supply train and burned 63 wagons. "Personable," is the word Parker used to describe the personality of a recruiting officer in 1863. "He would have had to be professional, honest, and have to believe in what he was doing," he added. Parker than asked, "if there was no Confederate threat in 1863, who is he signing up to defend?

---

2. Trinidad Gallegos, interview with author, Watrous, NM, September 24, 2024.

Who is he signing up to fight?"[3] We'll return to this important question in a later letter.

"A good communicator, a good listener, someone who is up for adventure, who works independently, believes in what he's doing, the best salesperson he has to be, and believes this is a path," said Eric Carpio, chief community museum officer at History Colorado and director of Fort Garland Museum & Cultural Center, at Fort Garland, CO.[4]

Em does not return to Kansas, but his mother does.

This may be the first reference by Silas that he lacks the capacity to save money, even with his pay increase, but it won't be the last. He writes a lot about this in 1864, plus several other personal challenges that I suspect will leave the reader with a smile.

Written back in his beloved Central City, this letter is the last written from Gilpin County. He doesn't write again about his travels back and forth along the mountain trail outside of Golden, from Denver and Camp Weld to the tent towns of Missourie City, and Mountain City. Nothing is left in these mountain towns today that Silas would have known or seen on his travels, but the landscape he saw on the trail, the forests and the mountain peaks, from Golden, on the Golden Gate Canyon Road to Black Hawk, is still the same.

We read more of his longing to be home in Kansas in this letter. He wants to be with his family. This longing to be closer to family is a yearning many of us can relate to, whether we are close like Silas' family, or not, or located close by, or distanced by states or countries. We'll read of more longings to return to Lawrence in Silas' letters in the next year, 1864.

---

3. Byron Parker, interview with author, Pecos, NM, September 23, 2024.
4. Eric Carpio, interview with author, Fort Garland, CO, October 17, 2024.

Chapter Six
The Letters, Winter-Spring 1864 - From Fort Garland to Fort Lyon, Their World is About to Mightily Change

The first letter in the collection written to Chivington, Methodist minister and commander of the Colorado Regiment begins the New Year. Silas has been under Chivington's command for the last two years. He is still assigned to recruiting service, and as we see in this first letter his voice advocating for the men, is a loud voice of justice.

Letter Nine
to Colonel John Chivington

January 3rd, 1864
Fort Garland, Colorado Territory

Colonel,

After a very tedious journey I have arrived at Fort Garland. I could get no kind of an animal at Pueblo so had to go to Shoup's camp by coach, arrived there at noon, procured a horse and one soldier. By the way, I got the soldier to reenlist before I left camp besides four or five others. I arrived at Doyle's Ranch on the Hurfano [sic] at dark. One of the horses took sick I left him and procured a mule and rode all night, snow was deep, weather cold and no trail to follow. Suffered considerably. Arrived at Royce's Ranch at five o'clock in the morning then rode to San Duvals and as it was then eleven o'clock yesterday morning. I went to bed to recuperate and started early this morning and arrived here at sundown. You can have some idea of my trip over the range. The snow was fifteen foot deep in some places and wind blowing snow so I could hardly see ten feet ahead of me. I got frost bit a little, none to hurt, though now I suppose you are tired of reading this report I will come to business.

I found Capt. Shaffer doing every thing possable [sic] for anyone to do with the pressure of all the 1st Regt officers of the Post against him. I have been to Co. E's Quarters to night and got Lt. Moore to accompany us for Political effect and am satisfied from remarks he made that he has done and is doing everything in his power (in such a way that it is hard to get a hold of him) to discourage reenlistments. And I am informed by Capt. Schaffer that the feeling of all the other officers are the same. In fact I can see it the little time I have been here. One remark Moore made to his men to night will give you some idea of him. I told the men that you did not think that veterans would have to serve three years and he up and told them that their own judgements were as good if not better than Col. Chivington's. It is plain to see that he is down on you and both he and the rest of our officers here as near as I can see are somewhat jealous of Shaffer and myself and some other officers thinking perhaps that there is a conspiricy [sic] to have them left in the shade in the organization of this Veterans Corps. Now Col., this is confidential when I tell you that I think there are some Girls at this post. I shall start for Conehos [sic] in the morning. I will have to go horseback as I can get no other conveyance. I dread it for I am so sore I can hardly walk. I will do every thing I can there and start back as soon as I can.

I am, Col., with much respect
Your Obt Servt
S.S. Soule
1st Lt., Cav of Col

-Military Records, National Archives

***

This letter describes the incredible hardships of traveling in the 19th century in Colorado Territory winters from blinding and blowing snow, frigid temperatures, and no trail to follow. In this letter, he describes the hardship of traveling in the winter, on a mule, and how it takes its toll on his body with frostbite, exhaustion, and that he can barely walk a day later after his arrival. I believe this was a three-day journey and this is how he started the New Year of 1864.

Riding a mule through 15 feet of snow, with windblown falling snow and no trail to follow, over mountain passes to get to Fort Garland had to be some of the most extreme physical challenges Silas faced in his military career. He arrives with frost bite and could barely walk. "Suffered considerable" seems like an understatement, especially because we rarely read in his letters any descriptions of the physical challenges of soldiering that he faced. And he continues to do his recruiting, reupping or reenlisting, even reenlisting the soldier who accompanies him on this harrowing journey. At Huerfano, which doesn't exist today, he might have seen the Spanish Peaks if the snowstorm didn't block them from sight. Today, pilgrims travel over LaVeta Pass, from Walsenburg to Fort Garland, a climb to 9,000 feet, instead of the trail he took, the Sangre de Cristo Pass. Snow wasn't on the road when I traveled over LaVeta Pass on my pilgrimage in

September, but I could see snow on adjacent peaks as the low cloud cover hung over, and not just a scattering but significant accumulation.

Clearly, Silas finds himself at Fort Garland facing some challenges to re-enlist because of rank, hierarchy, and some big personalities at the fort. Lt. Moore (1st Lt. William B Moore) is discouraging enlistments. There is confusion about when veterans need to enlist, and how. There's some back talk about Chivington, which Silas names to the colonel. We'll see him naming names again, but he has the sense, confirmed by Captain Schaeffer (Captain James R. Schaeffer), that the other officers at the garrison are discouraging enlistments.[1]

Just a few short months before Silas writes this letter, his old friend Boston abolitionist Lt. Col. Samuel Tappan was appointed as commander of Fort Garland. And finally, what does he mean by "there are Girls at this post." Is he outing women prostitutes? And if so, why?

Today, Fort Garland Museum & Cultural Center is located in the historic San Luis Valley where some of the very first towns in the Colorado Territory, like San Luis, was founded in 1851.

Mount Blanca, one of the four sacred mountains of the Dine (Navajo), is directly north of Fort Garland. To the east lies the snow-covered, Sangre de Cristo Mountain Range that Silas crossed in this snowstorm, that I saw on my pilgrimage. The vistas in the San Luis Valley today – the valley that extends miles to the south and west – are the very same views that Silas saw while traveling. He stayed at Fort Garland during this trip and went back and forth to Conejos for sev-

---

1. Officer identifications found in Fort Garland, Colo. August 1853-Dec. 1872 Returns from U.S. Military Posts, 1800-1916, National Archives, Family Search. accessed December 18, 2024, https://www.familysearch.org/search/catalog/589910

eral months as we will discover in his letters. It was home to officers, enlisted men, and a bed for visitors like Silas.

Instead of the story of former post commander Kit Carson, who was the officer who led the Dine (Navajo) on the forced Long Walk to Bosque Redondo, the storytelling these days at Fort Garland is quite different. It includes an exhibit illustrating a detailed system of Dine (Navajo) enslavement of women and children in the 1860s in Conejos at the home of Lafayette Head, the Ute Indian Agency agent, who also owned Dine (Navajo) enslaved people. It's a museum that tells the story of Buffalo Soldiers who were stationed at Fort Garland after the Civil War, not with simply photos, military records and narratives, but with art, and art made in community, curated by nationally recognized artist and photographer Chip Thomas, known for his Painted Desert Project on the Navajo Nation.[2]

Eric Carpio (Chicano), the chief community museum officer at History Colorado and director at Fort Garland Museum and Cultural Center, has begun offering listening sessions with descendants, consultations, and memory workshops to, in part, to name the trauma of storytelling that is complicated in the San Luis Valley of Hispanos, Dine, (Navajo), and Blacks. "These are the ways to name the need for healing and reconciliation," said Eric in an interview in his office inside the fort where the wooden floor planks creak when walked upon. "We still get asked why are we still thinking about this, why haven't we gotten over it," but Carpio believes that the work of interpretation is, in part, to "comfort the afflicted, and afflict the comfortable."[3] He works with contrasts like contrasts of fort commanders like Carson and Samuel Tappan, who was a Boston abolitionist before coming to the

---

2. Chip Thomas and the Painted Desert Project, Contemporary Arts Center, Cincinnati, OH, accessed December 20, 2024, https://www.contemporary-artscenter.org/experience/exhibitions/2024/09/chip-thomas-and-the-painted-desert-project.
3. Eric Carpio, interview with author, Fort Garland, CO, October 17, 2024.

Colorado Territory and found himself in the American Civil War. A world of contrasts of storytelling about Ute and Dine (Navajo) people, the Hispano who lived in the San Luis Valley for generations, and the white settlers who were taking over and occupying historic land where so many traveled before their arrival.

We add the messy and complicated presence of the military at an isolated fort that is created to protect those white settlers, and it's a chemistry compound for conflict and abuse for those who have been living on the land for generations. Carpio, the curators, the community, and the Descendants are telling a new story for the 21st century, of a complicated and messy history by listening with others, being at the core of the new journey.

***

Letter Ten
to Colonel John Chivington

Feb 18th, 1864
Guadelupe Conejos, Colorado Territory

Colonel

I arrived at Fort Garland on Monday, stopped one day at Shoup's camp. Think I induced some to enlist. I thought it would not pay to stay there longer for Shoup can and will do all that can be done by any one. I think I will make a raise out of Fort Garland. I got all the Non Coms together night before last promised to take those who would enlist with me to Conejos as escort and to assist me in the work there. I got ten that night, three Non Coms and seven Privates. Col. Tappan detailed them to report to me. I will go back in two days think I will get a good many more. Tappan and Jacobs assist me all they can. I cannot say as much for Moore and Murphy. I think that the sooner Moore gets out of the service the better. You have no idea of the feeling of Company E. to a man towards Moore. I think I could get two thirds of the CO if they were sure that Moore would not command them, not one could be induced to enlist with him in command of them. He objected to my taking the men after they were detailed said he claimed the right to detail such men as he saw fit.

Now Colonel I wish to ask some questions which I trust you can answer by return mail. There is one man of Co. E who served in our Reg more than a year and was discharged honorably for disability which has since been removed and he enlisted again and was accepted. Can he re-enlist as a Veteran? There are two who have served five years in the Regulars and about a year in the 1st Cav of Colorado. Can they enlist? There is one who served four years in the Regulars. Then was Lt. in the New Mexican, was in the Battle at Valverde. Can he enlist? Another thing I can get more men if I can date their enlistments the same as Shaffer did, those he enlisted, the 1st of January. There are some men who lack a month or two of serving two years if they enlist when their time is up will the receive their bounty?

I am with much Respect,

Your Obt servt
S.S. Soule, 1st Lt
1st Cavalry of Col

To Col. J. M. Chivington, Cmdg Dist of Col
PS. Please write what news from Captain Wanless? What is my show? S.S.S.

-Military Records, National Archives

***

Conejos would have been a long day's ride from Fort Garland for Silas on a healthy horse. Heading south, Silas would have traveled on an angle towards Conejos from Fort Garland. He would have then headed south for the last leg of the ride. Winters in the San Luis Valley where he was traveling can be harsh with snow and freezing temperatures at night that would then warm up during the winter day.

We read in this letter, like the one before, Silas' continual advocacy for the men who are trying to re-enlist and purposely advocating on their behalf. Some men assigned to serve in recruiting, are not as thorough and detailed as Silas, but isn't this the kind of soldier the military would like to see in the field, recruiting? There's no question that he takes his role as recruiter seriously. He's someone in military service who is deeply committed to his work and questions the policies of recruiting. Who can be recruited? What can be done to accommodate soldiers who may be two months shy of service, and will they get their bounty, in spite of? We see in this letter his humanity in a system that is not considered humane most of the time, but especially in 19th century military life in the Colorado Territory during the American Civil War where Confederates will most likely not return. Questioning the system is part of his advocacy for the men whom he serves with and hopes to continue recruiting and serving with into the future. In winter 1864, Col. Tappan is asking questions about Dine (Navajo) enslavement. Remember, he comes to Colorado as a Boston abolitionist doing all he can to dismantle the system of enslavement and the selling of human bodies.

What is Silas doing in Conejos? He gets permission to have escorts with him "and to assist me in the work there," but what is the work there? Samuel Tappan writes about the pilfering of provisions at Conejos by Ute Indian Agent Lafayette Head, and "tensions are at their highest."[4] But Carpio doesn't know why the military, and specifically Silas, is traveling back and forth, and working in Conejos. Neither does historian Virginia Sanchez, who literally wrote the book of Hispano history and culture in the San Luis Valley during Territorial Colorado.[5]

"What we do know is that the citizens had petitioned for Lafayette Head's removal."[6] The time of that citizen petition is exactly when Silas is crisscrossing the San Luis Valley, after he arrived at Fort Garland on January 3, following the horrendous travel adventure crossing the Sangre de Cristo Mountain Range in the previous letter. The Hispano citizens from Conejos filed a petition to the Territory's attorney general, Samuel Brown, on January 18 to replace Head, who they considered the cause of raids by some hungry Indigenous bands in his jurisdiction. "They considered Agent Head the cause of all the troubles and difficulties... the people [had] been subject to for these last two years."[7]

The mystery continues in that there is no mention of Silas in any of the January, February, or March 1864 lists of "Commissioned Officers, Present and Accounted For" at Fort Garland or mentioned in the "Record of Events" for each of those months.[8] The "Record of Events" documents the comings and goings of military officers visiting the fort.

These letters to Chivington and his mom from Fort Garland and Conejos are the only words that set Silas' presence in the

---

4. Carpio, 2024.
5. Virginia Sanchez, *Pleas and Petitions, Hispano Culture and Legislative Conflict in Territorial Colorado*, (Louisville, CO: University Press, 2020).
6. Virginia Sanchez, phone interview with author, November 25, 2024.
7. Sanchez, *Pleas and Petitions*, 145.
8. Fort Garland, Aug. 1855-Dec. 1872, Returns from U.S. Military Posts, 1800-1916.

San Luis Valley, and traveling back and forth in the frigid and wintery conditions that yield into cold and spring conditions. He writes he has an escort with him, but not in every letter. He writes that he gets mail in Conejos in the next letter to his mom, which sounds like he has a somewhat permanent address, but there is no address.

We don't know where he sleeps when he's in Conejos. And we don't know the details of what he's doing there. As I look back in rereading these letters over and over, I'm reminded that he doesn't mention where he sleeps on these trips and rarely mentions the specifics of his work. In some previous letters he does, but not always. I've had to remind myself that in these letters, as a recruiting officer, he works very independently, and maybe no one knows or is informed of the details of his overnights or travel.

Maybe I simply need to admit that this mystery of what he is doing in Conejos is going to remain a mystery. Lest I forget that these letters he writes to his mom, while frequently includes the details of everyday living, leaves out a lot of the details around work. Maybe it's intentional that he doesn't want her to know and worry, maybe he doesn't have the time to write all the details, but we don't know. Maybe there have been times in your life, reader, that you didn't write the details of your life in a letter to your mom!

***

Letter Eleven
to his mother, Sophia

February 22nd, 1864
Guadeloupe Conejos County,
Colorado Territory

Dear Mother

I received a letter from you this morning, the first I have had for a long time. I should have answered you[r] last letter but I have not written to any body for so long that I have forgotten how. Besides I have been busy on recruiting services and as I have been well and hearty, thought it would make no difference. I am now down to the edge of New Mexico but will return to denver [sic] in a few days when I am in hopes to get a Lt Colonel's Commission to go to Idahoe [sic] Ter[ritory] to assist in raising a new Regiment. I now have a Capt['s] Commission but have no money, having spent it on Recruiting service, but will have some soon and if you want any let me know and I will raise it for you. Our luck was not very good in Kansas, but we will not know the difference ten years from now. I got a letter from Will a few weeks ago but have not answered it. I have not heard from Em or Annie for a long time. I suppose Lawrence is built up again most as good as new. Mrs. Boynton has gone back to Kansas. Stearn's folks are still at Central doing well I think.

Geo Cutter is out in Idaho Ter[ritory] but is not doing much I think. I keep on in the even tenor of my ways enjoying myself all the time. Whether I am strapped or have plenty of money it makes no difference to me. I hope you don't have the blues any more but I expect you do. Don't you wish you was as contented as me. We had a funeral here yesterday. Two of the soldiers of my escort got in a row with some Mexicans a night or two ago and one soldier and two Mexicans was wounded. The soldier is dead and I think one of the Mexicans will pass in his checks in a few days. Now I don't know Mother as I can write anything that will interest you in the least. I suppose all you want to know from this country is that I am well and getting along first rate. If I don't go to Idaho I will try and get a furlough and give you a visit in the spring. If I do perhaps Annie will come to Kansas with me. I hope her eyes will get well. Give my love to all the folks. How are our Woolwich relations?

Your Sonny wonny,

Sile

Direct to Denver as before. Sile

-Anne E. Hemphill Collection

***

A letter of assurance to his mom that "I am well and getting along first rate," but we also read that there's been a death of a soldier in his escort. All may not be as well as he describes in this letter. He is back in Conejos, where he would be hearing many languages at this center of the world just north of the New Mexico-Colorado line. He would hear the language of the Dine (Navajo) and the Ute, and Spanish, maybe sometimes interpreted for him, sometimes not.

He writes of hope that Lawrence is recovering and healing from Quantrill's Raid in August and writes of hope for his mom that she no longer "has the blues." The word he gives himself is content and "enjoying myself all the time whether I am strapped or have plenty of money it makes no difference to me." Writing about money, the lack of it, or the plentiful of it, is a common refrain in Silas' letters.

A lieutenant colonel's commission to the Idaho Territory does not happen and I imagine that this possibility came only about through his old friend George Cutter, who himself is in Idaho. He doesn't get a furlough to come home to Kansas, either. His longing to return tugs at my heartstrings. The Woolwich relations refer to his ancestral home in Woolwich, ME, the town where his dad, Amasa was born to Samuel and Joanna Soule. Silas' mom, Sophia (Low) was born to William and Mary Low, next door in Bath, ME, so when we read of Woolwich or Bath in Silas' letters, he is connecting not only with aunts, uncles and cousins to the page, but the ancestral home of Soule's and Low's. There is much travel between Lawrence and Bath-Woolwich for Silas' siblings and mom, and not a simple feat in the 19th century. That commitment to travel though, demonstrates the deep connection that his family has to Maine, and the need to keep that connection alive face-to-face with seeing each other. As we read in Silas' letter to Thayer and Eldridge, returning home to Lawrence from Boston was quite the journey, imagine Maine.

This is his last letter written from Conejos. Besides the home of the Ute Indian Agent Lafayette Head, there is not much in Conejos today, except the oldest church in Colorado. Silas would have seen both the Lafayette Head house and Our Lady of Guadalupe Catholic Church founded in 1858. Today, after several new constructions, a fire, a rebuild, and a new addition, the church of 1864 is long gone. The church is two blocks away from Head's house which today is in disrepair and neglect and was placed on the Endangered Places List by Colorado Preservation Inc. in 2021.[9]

In my pilgrimages, I've observed that preservation of 19th century buildings I've visited in Kansas, New Mexico, and Colorado vary from story to story, history to history but also from commitment to commitment to preserve them. And

---

9. Colorado Preservation Inc., accessed December 25, 2024, https://www.coloradopreservation.org/2021-colorados-most-endangered-places/.

isn't preserving buildings part of honoring them, remembering them, or even memorializing those who lived or worked in them? One has to wonder, how do our historic sites determine what historical buildings get saved and preserved, and what doesn't? The adobe buildings at Fort Craig have been disintegrating over generations. Fort Union has bricks and fireplaces that still stand, but so much is now eroding back into the land, and so much was already taken before the property came under the care of the National Park Service. These are monuments to something that is lost.

I discovered on this New Mexico pilgrimage the monument-marker in Santa Fe, NM that says there was an internment camp just east of the monument that housed 4,000 American men of Japanese descent, between 1942 and 1946. This public monument, located in a dog park, that one has to meander through neighborhoods to get to, is the only public recognition of the internment camp.

How we honor with memorials, how we recall history with preserved buildings or skeletons of buildings, require not just historic preservationists, but it requires an effort to listen to community, to be community to each other when historic buildings need our help. We need community to create monuments, memorials, as well as care for them, and update them with new language when needed. We need leaders to listen to community when language on monuments needs to be revised, as in the Battle of Peralta monument in the Santa Fe Plaza. Community had been telling the city for decades about the inappropriate language on the panel that calls Indigenous people "savages."[10]

My takeaway from Eric Carpio, at Fort Garland, is that community needs to be invited, and show up when museum

---

10. John C. Bienvenu, "Making Sense of Santa Fe's Soldiers Monument: Part One," August 25, 2022, accessed December 25, 2024, https://bienvenu-law.com/2022/08/25/making-sense-of-santa-fes-soldiers-monument/.

exhibits are being imagined. We gather stories in this listening, of stories that are needing to be told, like the Santa Fe Internment Camp, the Soldier's Monument in the Santa Fe Plaza that was toppled, and the surprise of a Confederate marker in the middle of central New Mexico, near a well-traveled highway on land that is owned by Ted Turner.

We all need to participate in the telling of our stories of our diverse cultures – our past, our ancestors, our food, our rituals, customs, and ceremonies, the essence of who we are – when museums, libraries, and historical places tell stories interpreting the past.

I'll also note here, that in telling the story of diverse people in history, historical sites need to commit to hiring storytellers of color to interpret these stories of the past. If these sites want more visitors, and they do, then families of color need to see themselves reflected in the interpreters of the present. Rarely did I see a person of color at any of the pilgrimage sites I visited.

***

Letter Twelve
to Unknown Recipient

April 7th, 1864
Fort Garland, Colorado Territory

Sir

I have the honor to acknoledge [sic] the receipt of your letter from Hd Qtrs dated March 29th/64 and am surprised that you have not received any official letter from me at Hd Qtrs for I have sent three directed to the aaa Genl and two directed to the Col Commanding Dist one of which was marked official Business.

The Paymaster has not arrived nor have I heard any thing of his whereabouts although I sent him an express to try and urge him to be here by the 1st of April as it was utterly impossible to enlist any more Veterans until he arrived and I feared we would have trouble to get some mustered in who have already enlisted on account of false inducements held out to them which have not been complied with. He did not even answer my letter and I had but little hope to offer on the 1st of April as I have been assuring them every [day] that by the next mail I would surely get something definitive from Hd Qtrs in regard to the Paymaster. I asked in my letter to you for instructions. I am very eager to return to Denver as all my papers are there and my returns cannot be made out until I go back. Besides doing business in Central City which I could not settle when I left. I have no order to return and was in hopes you would have sent one by last mail.

When I came down I furnished my own conveyance to Camp Fillmore and procured horses of Lt. Shoup. I would like for instructions how to proceed back I would prefer to go by coach from Pueblo.

I am glad to learn that the Colonel retains command of the District and hope he will have arrived by the time you receive this. Tell him that if there ever was a mortal tired of a place and that Ft Garland, I am the man. Every thing is dull and the wind and snow blow continually and I am not remarkably pleased with the officers as a body at this Post do not forget to send me an order by return mail. I should have started back at the expiration of the extended time for enlisting Veterans had not the Colonel told me when I left Denver to be shure [sic] to be here when Fillmore arrived although I am satisfied that he had no idea that it would be the middle of April before his arrival.

I am with much respect,

Your obt Servt
SSSoule
1st Lt Cav of Col Recruiting Officer

PS
Please request the Colonel to see about my interest in obtaining a Captaincy as I have waited until my clothes are about worn out. SSS

-Military Records, National Archives

***

The snow and wind are blowing in the spring of 1864 at Fort Garland, as Silas finds himself lamenting a missing paymaster, which has thrown a wrench in his ability to do his job... "and it's utterly impossible to enlist any more Veterans until he arrives" and conversely, men can't get mustered out either. His expressions of concern about the ability of soldiers' reenlisting and mustering out is yet another call for justice for the men who he serves with, and in addition, the injustice that nobody is getting paid.

Sounds like he has been at Fort Garland for some time, maybe weeks, as "if there ever was a mortal tired of a place and that [is] Fort Garland, I am the man. Everything is dull and the wind and snow blow continually, and I am not remarkably pleased with the officers as a body at this Post." According to his individual muster-out roll dated April 14, 1864, at Fort Garland, Silas hasn't been paid since December 31, 1863. There is much to lament at Fort Garland in spring 1864.

This letter continues the pattern of traveling, and the independence he has demonstrated as he moves between Denver, Fort Garland, and soon, will be traveling southeast in the Colorado Territory to Fort Lyon.

Craig Haggit has a dream job if you love historical maps. As the maps and geospatial librarian at the special collections and archives at Denver Public Library, his expertise had no bounds when I visited him at the Denver Central Library. Tucked in the many little spaces historical maps can be found on the fifth floor, Haggit knows this collection of trails, roads, railroads, waterways and rivers, and so much more like the back of his hand. But more importantly, he knows how to make the connection between specific time periods in Colorado Territory history and the history of its cartography. Thanks to Haggit and the amazing Abby and Kelly in the manuscript room, I discovered maps found in original 1859 guidebooks written for the wayward gold miner, like Silas and the men from Coal Creek. These guidebooks helped those coming to Pikes Peak from "the States" on what to bring with them and pointed out the many directions to find gold.

So much travel has happened since those early 1860 days when Silas arrived in Denver on the Smoky Hill Road, then traveled to Golden, then on the Golden Gate Canyon Road to arrive in Black Hawk and all parts Gilpin County. The only letter that he specifically writes about landmarks along the way is the letter crossing the mountain pass, which was the Sangre de Cristo Mountain Range, which he connected with at Huerfano. Unfortunately, there are no details about the trails he rides from Fort Garland to Conejos, except on historic maps, the "Road to Fort Garland" is clearly marked from Conejos.

Trails are rarely named in Silas' letters, nor are they identified with a name on historic maps. We have to conclude that he maybe didn't have maps at all, just a well-worn trail that was meant to be followed. We can clearly see that there is a trail from Camp Weld to Raton Pass, and to Fort Union, NM, but the only path is to follow a line, and not a name. The same is true from Fort Union, to Santa Fe, to Albuquerque, to Socorro, and then to Fort Craig, Silas' most southern destination, travelling well into central New Mexico. The most distinctive trail in many of the southern Colorado-northern New Mexico maps is the historic Santa Fe Trail, which Silas traveled on from Raton Pass to Fort Union, NM, and then again to where Colorado soldiers fought the Confederates at the Battle of Glorietta Pass, north of Santa Fe, NM.

I was pointed to several drawers of maps on the fifth floor of the Central library that honestly, when opened, reminded me of a very embedded deep childhood memory of the smell of my grandfather's desk when I opened his cavernous desk drawers as a child. These map drawers, unlike my grandfather's desk drawers, held a cartographer's... and everyone who loves maps... joy. Maps of all make, era, colors by county, regional, with trail names, and no trail names. Deep in the bowels of the collection, where no mere mortal like me is allowed, came the rare maps, many of them the size of the huge table I was sprawled over to find the location I was seeking with my trusted library-supplied magnifying glass.

Today, Google maps has pre-empted the paper map that I grew up with. Even MapQuest has now gone by the wayside. There is something of a touchstone with a paper state map, after you pull over on the side of the road with a cup of coffee, trying to figure out what's ahead.

Highways are our well-worn trails that get us where we need to go today, but the pilgrimage invitation for me was always to try and get on a dirt road. Maybe that's your invitation, too.

***

Letter Thirteen
to his mother, Sophia

June 2nd, 1864
Camp Fillmore

Dear Mother

I know you are worrying about me because I have not written for so long but I am getting out of the notion of writing and have been busy for the last month fixing up my papers. And just as I got them fixed, my office was swept away by the flood and I lost everything. I had papers, letters, clothing, and all. Wasn't I in luck. Blessed are the poor for they have nothing to lose. I am now in command of my Company, a hundred brave warriors. Ain't I proud. I am on my way to Fort Lyon. I do not know where I shall go from there. I may go to fight Indians. If I do, I will write first so you can be worrying while I am gone.

I received a letter from Em a short time ago. She told me that you was going to stay a while in Bangor. I would send you some money by this mail but am afraid to as the Indians are bad along the road and may take the coach. I will send some the first safe opportunity. One of my men was killed and two wounded in an Indian fight last week. I don't know what more to write. There is nothing I know of that would interest you. I still suffer with pleasure. Give my love to all the folks and when you write let me know how you and the Girls get along, if you need money, etc.

I have some claims in the mountains that I could have sold a few weeks ago for then thousand dollars if I had been there but if they are worth anything they are worth $50,000.00. I think I can sell them for that much in a year from now if they work the mines as they have begun to and they pay as well. Lewis Tappan sold some he had for $500,000.00 just a half a million dollars. That was pretty good wasn't it? Who knows but we are rich? I own fifty mining claims and there ought to be some good ones and if one of them is good it is a fortune for any one. I will send you my photograph when I write again.

From your sonny

Sile

-Anne E. Hemphill Collection

***

Acknowledging the worry his mom must have about his safety, and the assurance that he is alright, is a common theme in Silas' letters to her, especially in letters where he writes about the deaths of his own soldiers. Obviously, there is every reason for her to worry, and in this letter, she reads for the first time, of floods.

The Cherry Creek Flood which Silas writes about to his mother was a deadly disaster that Denverites woke up to on the morning of May 20, 1864. Eight people died, but suspicions at the time indicate that there were many more, never accounted for.[11] He confirms in the next letter that indeed he was in Denver on May 20.

He writes this letter from Camp Fillmore, which was close to Pueblo in 1864.

---

11. Brian K. Trembath, "May 1864 Brought Denver's First Big Flood – and Swept Away Much More," Denver Public Library, May 20, 2020, accessed December 20, 2024, https://history.denverlibrary.org/news/denver/may-1864-brought-denvers-first-big-flood%E2%80%94and-swept-away-much-more history

"Blessed are the poor for they have nothing to lose!" is a sweet paraphrasing from The Beatitudes in Matthew 5:3-10 from the New Testament in the Bible. He has grown up in a Congregational tradition, so it's not totally a surprise that he is riffing on The Beatitudes and creating his own blessing. His family, and many others who traveled to Lawrence in the 1850s with the New England Emigrant Company, were Congregationalists from New England, the birthplace of Congregationalism in America. Silas, his parents, and these other Congregational families, founded Plymouth Congregational Church in 1854 and began worship in a sanctuary made of hay bales.[12] Silas' foundation in faith was most likely well-established prior to coming to Lawrence.

There will be more references in letters around his faith, but creating a blessing for himself, makes me suspect the reference to The Beatitudes is an important part of assuring his mom that he is safe and that there is nothing for her to fear. "I still suffer from pleasure," was probably every mother's hope to read in a letter from her soldier son in the American Civil War but Silas' reference is that he has all he needs.

He announces that he's headed to Fort Lyon and "I may go fight Indians." He doesn't fight Indians, but I'll invite us to pause here. Remember Byron Parker asked, "what is he recruiting for?" in those letters from late 1863 and early 1864.[13] There is no fear of Confederates, especially now. Has the last six months been about recruiting and reenlisting soldiers for what is to come with Cheyenne and Arapaho people? When he is at Fort Lyon, he is the closest he has come to the Cheyenne and Arapaho. We know he was present in Conejos with Ute and Dine (Navajo) people, Hispano people, but Fort

---

12. Plymouth Congregational Church, Lawrence, KS, accessed December 20, 2024, https://www.plymouthlawrence.com/.
13. Byron Parker, interview with author, Pecos, NM, September 23, 2024.

Lyon is very close to where the Arapaho and Cheyenne camp, not far from Smoky Hill.

In his book, *Massacre at Sand Creek*, historian Gary Roberts writes that in the spring of 1864, weeks before Silas writes this letter, the peace between Cheyenne and Arapaho, and Governor John Evans and the military in Colorado is beginning to unravel. Fueled by mostly rumors, some high-ranking military officials suggest that "everything indicates the commencement of an Indian war."[14] But, "on the other hand, several officers reported that the Cheyenne were frightened and anxious to maintain good relations with whites." Roberts concludes that "the evidence was far from convincing that a war was planned by the Cheyenne and Arapaho."

When Silas writes, "I may go fight Indians" in this letter, it must be because he is hearing of the friction in Denver, and the uneasiness it must feel for officers 200 miles away in isolated Fort Lyon.

But he is with commander of Fort Lyon Major Edward Wynkoop. Ned, who arrived at Fort Lyon as fort commander on May 8 is an old friend. While he has a few years on Silas, Ned is also from Kansas and was in the New England Emigrant Company that arrived in Lawrence in 1856. We will discover soon enough by the end of the summer of 1864, that Ned is becoming a peacemaker, with Silas, and Southern Cheyenne Chief Black Kettle.

Silas and Ned marched together 400 miles in 15 days to Fort Union. They fought together at Glorieta and Peralta. They've needed to trust one another in moments of battle. Their friendship already runs deep, but by the time autumn comes in just a few short months, their trust will grow deeper

---

14. Gary L. Roberts, *Massacre at Sand Creek, How Methodists Were Involved in an American Tragedy* (Nashville, TN: Abingdon, 2016), 108.

in the profound ways of seeking peace with Cheyenne and Arapaho chiefs.

***

Letter Fourteen
to his sister, Annie

June 17th, 1864
Fort Lyon, Colorado Territory

Dear Annie

I have just received a letter from you, and I was very glad to hear from you. I am in command of my company and like it very well. I have 94 men and get along very well with them. Fort Lyon is on the Arkansas River about 250 miles from Denver. I suppose you heard of the great flood we had in Denver. I was there. My Office was in a large two story Brick building. It was washed away and I did not save any thing out of it so you see I have been drove out as well as you. It was an awful flood. It tore down Churches and printing offices. In fact it washed away most a quarter of the City and drownded [sic] a number of men, women and children. We have had a good deal of rain this season. The Arkansas River is so high that it has come in the post and drove most of the Laundresses out.

I don't know what I shall do this summer but think will have some Indian fighting to do. Part of my company had a fight with them a week or two ago. I lost 2 killed and 3 wounded. They killed about 20 Indians. I have not been [in] any fight yet but may have a chance soon.

I don't know what to write that would interest you. I would send you some money to you but am afraid the

Indians will rob the Coach, but if you want any let me know and I will send some to you. I would like you to send some papers to me when you can. Em has not sent any for a long time. I got a letter from Mother a week or two ago and answered her. I have not had a letter from Will since he left Kansas. Give my love to all the folks. Tell them that I would like to hear from them. I think I shall go to Maine to marry so if you see any nice Girl who wants to be the wife of a Captain of a hundred <u>Braves</u> tell them that I am the man they are looking for.

Sile

-Anne E. Hemphill Collection

***

Historic Fort Lyon was located close to present day Lamar, and there is nothing left but native grass. No historic architecture remains, and no indication of the once thriving and diverse community of soldiers, laundresses, sutlers and musicians that made this home for so many.

There are three other historic forts where we've journeyed to; Fort Craig in southern New Mexico that is open for interpretation by the Bureau of Land Management six months out of the year but has no active historic preservation, Fort Union in northern New Mexico, managed by the National Park Service and is interpreted year-round with ongoing (but scaled down) historic preservation every summer of skeletal buildings still standing, and Fort Garland in southern Colorado, managed by Historic Colorado, interpreted year-round, and has an active historic preservation program for maintaining its buildings. The overwhelming challenges of limited resources and aging structures for preserving our architectural history, and the storytelling of the people who lived and worked in these buildings, continues to be a constant struggle in the American West.

He doesn't fight the Cheyenne and Arapaho.

As I reread this letter over and over, I'm struck by the way he's able to speak of violence with his sisters and mom. He's honest. Transparent. He wants them to know not only about his dreams of finding someone in Maine to marry, but that he is in a place that is dangerous.

While he is not in the fight, the murder of the Hungate family, Nathan, Ellen and their two daughters, Laura and Florence, on June 11, near present-day Elizabeth, CO, escalates an already tense environment in Denver. Their bodies were brought to Denver and put on display, which caused widespread panic.[15] Their murders will become the backdrop to the summer of wonder and worry, frantic and fear about impending violence, fueled by Evans and Chivington.[16]

It's been years since I searched out the Hungate family grave at historic Fairmount Cemetery, but since this is a book about how we remember, what is memorialization, and how does it all connect in our lives today, I went back to their stone. It's located in one of the oldest parts of the cemetery, and on this fall day, I was able to walk right to it on the dirt road, covered with fallen leaves. They were killed in 1864, and Fairmount didn't open until 1892, so this family was one of thousands, who were relocated from the original Denver cemetery, Mount Prospect Cemetery, near what is today Cheesman Park and the Denver Botanic Gardens. Many people who were relocated came to Fairmount, and many came to Riverside Cemetery, which was founded in 1876, the year Colo-

---

15. Sand Creek Timeline of events relating to the Sand Creek Massacre,1864, National Park Service, accessed December 20, 2024, https://www.nps.gov/sand/learn/timeline.htm.
16. Roberts, 111-112.

rado became a state. Silas' grave was one of those thousands of graves that was relocated to Riverside Cemetery. These oldest cemeteries are the final resting place for many who were Denver's first residents.

The family gravestone lists Nathan, Ellen, their two daughters with their birth dates and death date. The final line on their stone says, "Killed by Indians." Gravestones are for perpetuity, and this stone speaks volumes about the sentiment in Denver in the summer of 1864. Anger and rage have been fueled by rumors and mistruths.

Silas has every reason to believe that he may have the chance, which is an interesting choice of words, to fight with Cheyenne and Arapahos, who he believes would be the aggressor, the instigator of violence that needs to be contained. This belief will change by the time summer comes to an end, but for now, in June, he is ready for a fight.

The Cheyenne and Arapaho are not the aggressor.

Chapter Seven
The Letters, Summer-Fall 1864 - Witnessing Peace, Witnessing Death

Summer brings extraordinary changes to the Plains of the Colorado Territory unlike anything seen so far. We begin to see and hear voices we haven't seen or heard from, Governor John Evans, Cheyenne and Arapaho chiefs, Southern Cheyenne George Bent, and the times are changing rapidly. By the end of the year, life will be forever changed for the Cheyenne and Arapaho people for generations to come.

***

Letter Fifteen
to his sister, Annie

July 16th, 1864
Fort Lyon, Colorado Territory

Dear Annie

I just received a letter from you and was kinder glad to hear from you. I do not write as often as I used to but will answer letters as soon after receipt as I can. I am in Fort Lyon on the Arkansas River. There are five Companies here besides one section of Battery [artillery] and the Regtl Band. I have a good company and get along first rate. Yesterday at Dress parade the Major Comdg Post had orders read to the Battalion complimenting my Company on their military appearance and discipline, referring to them as an example for the troops at this Post. So you see I get along very well. I am the same Boy, Annie, as I used for to be. In fact I imagine that I am only 17 years old. We have been expecting to be ordered into the field for the last month and are still expecting to go on an Indian Campaign. I think I will like it better than laying at this Post for it is as hot as Blazes and the mosquitoes are very numerous and the[y] have got in the habit of biting.

I got a letter from Mother yesterday and will answer it today if possible. There is a man by the name of Hains here who will start for Bangor in the course of a week. He is acquainted with Stearns Lows folks and is going there. I think I had better send about $200 by him to Mother and if you want any of it perhaps she would give you some. I spend my money most as fast as I make it but when you are in need of some don't be bashful (for you know we used to be pretty well acquainted with one another) and let me know. I have not heard from Will since he left Lawrence. I am afraid he has been nipped in some of those fights in Tenn. You and Mother write for me to be a Christian and not be wild &c but the Army don't improve a fellow so much in that respect and you know I never was much of a Christian and am naturally wild, but I have seen so much of the world and are not much changed. I think there is not much danger of me spoiling. Our Col is a Methodist Preacher and whenever he sees my drinking, gambling, stealing or murdering he says he will write to Mother or my sister Annie so I have to go straight.

Give my regards to every body and write when convenient. I would like to get Bill's wife's photograph. Haven't you got one to send me? I have all the family but here and Em in an album. I send you one of mine taken rough without my uniform. Does it look like me? I have my hair shaved so close now that I look like a Penitentiary bird. I have a sure thing that the Indians cannot get my scalp.

Yours &c

Sile

-Anne E. Hemphill Collection

***

Letter writing as ritual. I just need to mention out loud that letter writing can be a ritual. The commitment to stay connected and the time it takes to write these letters to the family, AND for his mom and sisters to write as often as they do, speaks of family ritual to me. Finding the paper to write on, searching for the pen, sitting down in the fort, sitting outside in the backyard in Lawrence, or Bangor. Maybe having a cup strong coffee, or tea, or lemonade close by. The only way they can stay connected in the intimate way they all do is through words on a piece of paper. At some point, each of these women, his mom and his sisters, put each of their collections of letters from him, together. They have been passed down now for four generations, and because of Silas' descendants' spirit of generosity in sharing these family letters, the book you hold in your hands has been written.

Every time I read this letter out loud at Silas' grave, Pastor Dustin Adkins says, "he's more of a Christian than anyone I know." And every time, I smile. A Disciples of Christ pastor for 30 years, he knows a thing or two about who professes to be a Christian, and is, or isn't.

We met up recently in his Denver church office, where the fake fire in the fireplace blazed and we drank coffee. Fairly new to this United Church of Christ church, he is aware that the faith community where he serves is a parish where hospitality runs deep, and the commitment to feeding hungry people is part of this church's origin story.

From childhood, Adkins, a white, gay man, made intimate connections with stories that family members told, and especially with his grandfather, who was a great storyteller. Though he hasn't heard those childhood stories from his grandfather in more than 35 years, "I carry an emotional portrait of this man and awareness of how he influenced my life. Historically, we don't get this three-dimensional wallflower of history, but then there are those people who are truly exceptional through their stories. I think Silas is one of those for me."[1]

He says curiosity drew him to his first visit to Silas' grave to hear me read the letters out loud on his July birth day for the first time. "I had curiosity about this new, random friend and a curiosity talking about the stories of this soldier. It was such an oddball thing; I had to go. I wasn't expecting to fall in love with the idea of Silas."

There is something real about him, he added. In these letters, there is nothing fake or presumptive. He described Silas as a brilliant writer. "His writing and experiences have a warmth we can relate to and a beauty in his connection with others." It's in the place of community, his family, friends, and colleagues, that Adkins sees Silas as a natural leader.

---

1. Dustin Adkins, interview, Denver, CO, December 19, 2024.

The line "that I never was much of a Christian" doesn't remind him of a traditional religiosity, "he's certainly not pious." But Adkins does see a man of faith. "People say to me sometimes, you're a pastor, preaching, and saying and do the Lord's work, and they think of that as the way. Religion has brainwashed us into thinking that is Christianity. But that's not what Christianity is about. In every expression of his being I hear his commitment to justice, which is exceptional. There are people who are justice, everything exudes justice. And with everything they are and everything they do; they live out a call to love your neighbor and stand up with the oppressed.

"What could be more Christian than by putting your life on the line for the benefit of others?"

Knowing Silas through these letters, Adkins feels that it's Silas' family, friends, and community, beginning in his childhood that is the great teacher of his faith. "Their commitment to justice and dismantling enslavement goes well beyond thoughts, it's a faith predicated by action.

"Anytime we encounter these letters, I experience a deep grief about knowing what's coming. Not just the Massacre, but what's coming for Silas. We all know people that know the right thing, and Silas is one of those... his is the product of our raising, our faith."

The line about the "Methodist preacher" "who is pious about stealing and murdering," and who Adkins reminded me of is the very thing that Silas writes about, Chivington does four months after this letter is written. Still, in this July letter there is a sign of respect.

Because he knows these letters so well, Adkins has struggled with the idea that only two soldiers out of the 600 that day of the Massacre disobeyed orders and wonders out loud if there had to be more men who felt like Joe (Lt. Joseph Cramer) and Silas, "but we fall prey to following the crowd, compromising our moral compass, decisions, and values, even if we'd like to think we couldn't.

"I think how lonely it must have been... to feel so clearly to be morally right and be left alone." When I asked him if there were others in history that he felt were like that... clearly understanding what is right, doing right, and then being alone... he quickly said "Dietrich Bonhoeffer."

When pressed about how these two men who lived in different centuries, countries, and faiths, with how are they alike, Adkins replied that it's the parallel of their immense moral courage, and added that their decisions were not made in an absence of fear, but instead that these two men had to know the risks of speaking out to the events they saw happening. "There are people in the world who are firemen, people who walk into a fire, and everyone else is running out. Silas and Dietrich go into the fire knowing things have to be said."

Bonhoeffer was a German Lutheran pastor and theologian who was a vocal part of the anti-Nazi resistance. He was arrested in April 1943, transferred to Flossenburg concentration camp, and was executed by hanging on April 9, 1945, with liberation only days away. He was 39 years old. Of all his writings, *The Cost of Discipleship* is the most well-known and is considered a modern-day classic for Christian theologians on what does it means to follow Christ, especially in a world where a dangerous and criminal government leads.

"So often we turn our eyes from injustice because it's painful or we don't know what to do with it. I ask, how do we bring about justice through violence,?" asks Adkins.

"Imagine how hard it was for him that he couldn't stop the Sand Creek Massacre."

With days left before one of the busiest times of the liturgical year for a pastor, we said our goodbyes. As we walked to the church parking lot, I remembered Adkins told me a few weeks earlier that he would bring pie to next year's letter reading at Silas' grave in July. The idea of eating pie in community in the cemetery with others who love Silas as much as I do, filled my heart with gladness and peace. In a broken world that needs so much more gladness and peace, my prayer is that we eat more pie at the grave together.

***

Letter Sixteen
to his mother, Sophia

July 29th, 1864
Fort Lyon, Colorado Territory

Dear Mother,

I received a letter from you last week and should have answered it before but expected that Mr. Haynes would start every day and I wanted to send it as he is going right to Bangor. I send you two hundred dollars in Green backs by him thinking it will be safer than the mail for it is rather risky sending money east now for the Indians and Guerellers [sic] are plenty on the road. I find it is no use for me to try and save any money in the Army without I send it to you for I spend all I get. In fact it costs about two dollars a day to live without spending money foolishly and when I have money you know I don't care much about expenses so I guess I will send some every pay day after paying my debts and go on tick. I want you to spend money when I send it to you as though it did not cost anything. Get good clothes and live well for if you don't spend it I will. All I care for is to have part of the farm in Kansas to live on when I get out of the service. I suppose I shall be in three years longer. I like it and I will enjoy myself hugely if I can only send you money enough to live comfortable. I think I shall go down and see you next winter on furlough.

I wrote to Annie last week. I don't think she had best go to Kansas at present as I expect there will be more fighting in Kansas this fall than there ever was before. They are fortifying Leavenworth now. Price's army is disbanded and I believe they will play a lively string bush wacking the borders of Missourie[sic] and Kansas. I got a letter a week or two from Em and answered it. Did she get the photograph? Would you know that it was me? I am still at Lyon and expect to remain but cannot tell. We have sent five Cos after Indians and left three Cos at this Post. I expect Major Wynkoop will go to Denver in a day or two. If he does I shall be in command of the post. Won't I put on style! I suppose you think I spend a good deal of money, but when you consider that it costs sixty dollars for a coat, twenty for a pr of pants, sixteen for a pr of boots, ten for a hat, and six and a half apiece for shirts it counts up. And you know a Captain has to wear good clothes.

I had a birth day the 26th, I suppose you know I am 26 years old, most old enough to marry, ain't I? Well, it is late and the mosquitoes are troublesome. I guess I will close. I went to a show tonight and saw a man turn his joints out of shape for a dollar so you see we are quite civilized in this country. Give my love to every body and tell them that I should be glad to hear from them. Don't fret if you don't hear from me once a year for if I get killed you will hear of it soon enough. I have not heard from Will for a long time. I don't know where to write and if I did I don't suppose he would get it.

Your Sonny Sile

-Anne E. Hemphill Collection

***

This letter solved a mystery for me that had lingered for a very long time. In the photo of Camp Weld at Denver in September (it's coming up) where the Cheyenne and Arapaho chiefs sit for a photo with Ned and Silas, I have never quite believed that the person identified as Silas was indeed Silas. In every other photo I've seen, he has a head of hair, so I have been mightily suspicious and at times even out loud doubtful. When I read this letter over and over, it dawned on me that the hair cut he writes about in this July letter, is the hair cut we see in the photo in September. Connecting a letter with a photo. "Did you know it was me?" I'm a believer.

His own mortality, death and birth swirls around in this letter to his mom, like a wind that takes the fall leaves up in the air and lands them gently on the ground. We won't see this language of lifegiving and life ending in any other letter written by Silas. He holds them both... "for if I get killed you will hear of it soon enough," and "I had a birthday the 26th, I suppose you know. I am 26 years old, most old enough to marry, ain't I?"... with great tenderness as he writes to his mom. He hopes to return home to Kansas and marry, and yet he also knows enough to be pragmatic about being in the military at a very isolated fort, in an atmosphere of uncertainty where rumors are the stuff of decision-making in Denver. These are challenging times to hold hope and reality together in a letter, especially to his mother.

A month earlier, Evans issued, in his capacity of ex-officio Supt. of Indian Affairs for the Territory, a circular to the 'Friendly Indians of the Plains.' "Friendly Indians are directed to report to their nearest Indian agents, who will direct them to 'places of safety."[2] This was the latest attempt at the time to put fear into the hearts of the people of Denver, and the Territory, as there was not a threat to the citizenry by Cheyenne and Arapahos.

And this letter, like so many we've journeyed with covers some of the familiar writing subjects, money (or lack of it!), his hope to return to Kansas but thinks he'll be in the service for another three years, a prediction of upcoming fighting in Kansas and the fortification of Fort Leavenworth. Located on the Missouri-Kansas border, Fort Leavenworth was a training station for Kansas volunteers in the Civil War and because of its location was vulnerable to Confederates crossing the border.

But this letter includes some new language, an update on the structure of the operations of Fort Lyon, with the news that Silas would be commander of the Post in the absence of Major Wynkoop, and the expense to maintain his wardrobe. These are some of the most intimate daily details of his life that his letters are filled with and have been since his departure from home in 1860. He writes of travel, food, entertainment, weather, his life as an abolitionist, his daily life as a miner, and then later as a soldier. He likes getting letters and writes back quickly. He enjoys reading newspapers that his sisters send him and asks them to send him more. Three variables may have contributed to his literacy, he grew up in the New England North. He is white. His parents were literate.

It's been almost four years since Sophia's husband, Amasa died. Silas writes to her in Bangor, ME, her ancestral home

---

2. A Timeline of events relating to the Sand Creek Massacre, 1864, accessed December 20, 2024, https://www.nps.gov/sand/learn/timeline.htm.

where she, her siblings and parents lived. There was lots of travel between Maine and Kansas in these letters, and not just Silas' mom to visit her siblings, but also her daughter, and Silas' sister Emily, as well. Based on her 1865 diary, Sophia loved to quilt, knit, make dresses, spin wool, visit friends, and helped friends with sick children. She was quite the reader and pie, gingerbread and bread baker. She went to meeting most every Sunday.

And Will. A lament from a brother in a letter who doesn't know where Will is, hasn't heard from him, and is unsure if he would get his letter, even if he wrote. It sums up a lot of their relationship. Remember, it was Will who came to the Colorado Territory first, seeking gold and invited Silas to join him. None of the letters Silas wrote to Will were saved. Family means a great deal to Silas, and staying connected especially. We read about that connection in almost every letter he writes to his sisters and mom. His lament and longing for his brother, especially when he doesn't know if he would get a letter, even if he wrote, seems like a struggle for this younger brother.

***

Letter Seventeen
to his sister, Annie

August 15th, 1864
Fort Lyon, Colorado Territory

Dear Annie

I have just received a letter from you and hasten to answer it before I forget it. I am still at Fort Lyon and perhaps you had better direct your next here. I presume I shall be here some time yet. We have considerable trouble with the Indians, They would like to scalp us all. We have been chasing them for two weeks but only killed two. It is hard to get into a fight with them, they scatter so.

I wrote to Em today. I wrote to Mother last week and sent her two-hundred dollars in green backs by a man going to Bangor by the name of Haynes. He is acquainted with the Lows there. I expect to get a furlough and go down east in February but don't know. If I do and everything is quiet I would like to have you come out here with me. I think you would like it. I wish I had somebody to keep house for me, and you could make more money here than where you are. A school teacher of most any kind gets at least fifty dollars a month. I see workmen don't get near as much in the east as here for any common day laborer can get five dollars a day and get paid every night which is four dollars and board.

Money is not valued as it is in the states. If a fellow asks three or four to go into a oyster saloon and get supper it will cost from fifteen to 20 dollars especially if you eat what you want. Only think, fresh oysters. Come out packed in ice one dollar a dozen. I have sat down when I was hungry and wanted a good meal and eat four or five dozen but these things are luxuries. You cannot buy potatoes for less than eighteen or 20 cents a pound and I suppose you don't pay more than 4 or 5 dollars a bushel. If you want to buy anything in Colorado no one thinks of the price. I have often paid 25 cents for a glass of lemonade or beer. People are more liberal here than in the States. I wonder how I have managed to send Mother as much money as I have. For when we are among friends in Denver officers are supposed to be a jovial set and if you go into a saloon to take a drink if there are twenty strangers there you say Come Gentlemen and take something and everybody drinks something and your drink costs from five to ten dollars. I have seen men ask a crowd to drink and smoke and their bill would be as much as sixty dollars. Now I suppose you think we are a wicked extravagant people, but it is custom. You would think it strange down east to go in a Gentlemans house and have young ladies pass a decanter of whiskey to you. Well there is hardly an officer or any man of standing, especially a married man, who has not a decanter sitting on the table or beaureau [sic]. They would think it horrible in the states I suppose. Now I am just telling you some of the customs of the country to show the difference of customs.

Now I suppose you will ask is it possable]sic] that Sile drinks. I used to drink when I felt like it the same as every one else but I don't now for I bet sixty dollars against a $60 coat with the sutler that I would not take a drink for six months. It will be out the 26th of Jan. People don't get drunk as much here as in the states I think, and if they do nothing is thought of it. But you need not fret for me for I haven't been drunk and I expect it would take a gallon on to make me drunk.

Haven't I written a long letter for me? I did not think of any thing to write when I commenced and have not been ten minutes writing this. I have hardly taken my pen of[f] of the paper and I won't read it over for I am in a hurry to put this in the office. I received two papers by last mail which I expect you sent. I am much obliged to you and wish you'd send more. Well, good night.

Sile

Tell me what Sam Glass is doing and what Charley Cooms is doing.

-Anne E. Hemphill Collection

***

August 1864 was a complicated month for those at Fort Lyon and Silas' letter reflects this confusion in his military update, and in his life outside of the military in this letter. They almost need to counterbalance each of these two worlds. Between the last letter to his mom and this one to Annie, the men of Company D under the command of Silas, along with Company K and Company G, a total of 80 men and a howitzer go out to the field on August 7, as Ned was alerted to intelligence that a train had been attacked seven miles from the post. The soldiers spent two nights in the saddle, searching, even going to William Bent's ranch. They found a house that was "said to have been attacked by the Indians, which was unoccupied, but observed that there had been a conflict." Ned was "well convinced" that Satank, war chief of the Kiowas, was with a thousand more warriors of the Kiowas and Comanches and were located near the direction of Cimmaron. They were never found by the men of Fort Lyon.[3]

In August, the men of Fort Lyon participated in the Indian War of 1864 where escalated tensions led to attacks and reprisals from both sides, and while pursuing a band of Arapaho led by Arapaho Chief Neva, Lt. Joseph Cramer's horse threw him. He suffered a severe back injury. Cramer chased Neva with intent to fight and kill while Neva held back his men from annihilating the scattered troops because of his peace mission, as he was carrying a letter from several Cheyenne and Arapaho chiefs seeking peace.[4] George Bent wrote that

---

3. *The Rocky Mountain News*, August 27, 1864.
4. Joseph Cramer Biography, Sand Creek Massacre, National Park Service,

the Cheyenne raids during July and August, "were terrible affairs, but after all, the Indians were wild people in those days; they had been attacked again and again by the troops without any cause, and they were retaliating the only way they knew how."[5]

On August 11, Evans writes a second proclamation to "Citizens of Colorado" which authorizes citizens of the Colorado Territory to "kill and destroy, as enemies of the country, wherever they may be found...hostile Indians," and on the same day he receives authority from the War Department to raise a third regiment of volunteers for 100 days of service. The 3rd Regiment Colorado (US) Volunteer Cavalry is raised to "pursue, kill and destroy all hostile Indians that infest the Plains."[6]

The authority to recruit 100 volunteers from the War Department and Lt. Joseph Cramer chasing after Neva is a moment of historical confluence. It is the intersection of the American Civil War and the Indian War of 1864. The new recruits and the veterans.

He writes to Annie that "we have considerable trouble with the Indians – they would like to scalp us all," which is what he is being told by his commanders. "We have been chasing them for two weeks, but only killed two. It is hard to get into a fight with them, they scatter," appears that he is looking for the fight, he is chasing them to get into a fight. The Cheyenne and the Arapaho outside of Fort Lyon are not initiating the fight, the Colorado soldiers are.

He doesn't get the furlough in February he hoped for.

---

accessed December 20, 2024, https://www.npshistory.com/publications/sand/brochures/joseph-cramer.pdf.
5. George Hyde, edited by Savoie Lottinville, *Life of George Bent, Written From His Letters* (Norman, OK: University of Oklahoma, Norman, OK, 1968), 139.
6. Sand Creek Massacre Timeline, National Park Service.

And if we didn't know there was so much inflamed rhetoric in Denver by Evans, the sweet ethnology of his eating and drinking habits, he calls them "customs," would be downright delightful. And maybe that is the point. He is brushing off the current, and possibly impending "fights" with the Cheyenne and Arapaho, with delightful memories of life outside of the military setting he is in, and longingly reflecting about remembrances of a fellow "who asks three or four to go into a oyster saloon and get supper, it will cost from $15 to $20, especially if you eat what you want. Only think! Fresh oysters come out packed in ice, $1 a dozen. I have sat down when I was hungry and wanted a good meal and eat four or five dozen, but these things are luxuries." He writes of more pleasant Denver memories, of going into saloons, being in a gentleman's house "and have young ladies pass a decanter of whiskey." His declaration of not drinking any more over the bet of a coat with a sutler, is quite possibly a wakeup call about his drinking, rather than a bargain.

In some circles, we would call this grief talk. Sharing fond memories, interspersed with the tough, mysterious, unknown reality that he faces every day. This is his first adult "job" and he is now a captain in the military at an isolated fort, away from his tight family who he hasn't seen in close to four years and he thinks he could get killed. He's 26 years old. He dreams of getting married and returning to the Kansas farm. Who wouldn't have a sense of grief.

Unbeknownst to him, and between this letter and the next, much changes for Silas around the Cheyenne and Arapahos, beginning with George Bent, the son of trader William Bent and Owl Woman, a Cheyenne woman. Bent writes, "Late in August, while the young men were still busy raiding on the Platte, the chiefs called a council. Most of the older men in our camp were in favor of peace, although the young men were still raiding, and at this council it was decided to write to the authorities, ask for peace, and offer to give up the white prisoners who had been captured during the raids."[7] At the chief's dictation, Bent and his brother-in-law Edmund Guerrier who was also at this council, wrote two letters: one to Ned Wynkoop as the officer commanding Fort Lyon, and the other to Indian Agent Sam Colley, agent for the Cheyenne and Arapahos. Bent and Chief One Eye took the letter to Colley. And Eagle Head and Guerrier took Ned Wynkoop's letter, and according to Bent they were arrested by Ned, put in the guardhouse and were treated "very harshly."[8]

Ned, after releasing Bent and Guerrier, ultimately sees this as an opportunity to begin peace and free several white hostages, who the chiefs have offered in exchange for Cheyenne prisoners. On September 6 Ned rides out from Fort Lyon with 127 men, Silas included, to meet with Chief Black Kettle and other leaders on the Smoky Hill River. He described that there were "five hundred or six hundred warriors; their women and children were removed. He [Major Wynkoop] told them he wanted to talk to them and their chiefs came into our camp and held a council. Major Wynkoop asked them to give up the white prisoners in their possession. They said they were desirous of making peace with the whites. Major Wynkoop told them he had not the power to make peace, but if they would give up the white prisoners, he would take them to Denver before the governor and pledge himself to protect them to Denver and back; whether they made peace or not they should be safely returned." Silas said that "Black Kettle, their principal chief said the white prisoners were some distance from their camp and wanted us to move one or two days' march nearer Fort Lyon, and wait there two days and he would bring the white prisoners to us. They brought a white woman into our camp the same day, and the second day they brought in three children."[9]

---
7. Hyde, 142.
8. Ibid.
9. Silas Soule Testimony, February 15, 1865, 9.

They then went to Fort Lyon "with about fifty of their Indians, and from there to Denver with seven Indians and the captives."[10]

Evans and Chivington met with Cheyenne and Arapaho chiefs at Camp Weld on September 28, the same location where Silas wrote some of his first letters. Representing the Cheyenne were Black Kettle, White Antelope, and Bull Bear. Representing the Arapaho were Neva (whom Joe Cramer tried to chase down a month earlier), Bosse, Heaps of Buffalo and No-Ta-Nee.[11]

When they arrived, Silas said in his testimony, "Major Wynkoop asked the governor, Colonel Chivington and some others to meet in council at Camp Weld, to hear their propositions for peace. They had a talk with the chiefs. The Indians seemed very anxious to make peace. The governor told them that he could not make peace with them. They must look to military power for protection. Colonel Chivington told them that he left the matter with Major Wynkoop if they wanted peace they must come into the post and subject themselves to military law."[12]

They all returned to Fort Lyon where "Major Wynkoop told them to bring in the Indians of their tribe who were anxious for peace to Fort Lyon, and camp near the post, and he would immediately send to General Curtis and see if peace could not be made." Silas said that Ned sent Lieutenant Denison to General Curtis at Fort Riley, and the "Indians came in and complied with Wynkoop's orders and camped near the post."[13]

---

10. Ibid.
11. Sand Creek Timeline, National Park Service.
12. Silas Soule Testimony, 9.
13. Ibid.

George Bent writes that when Black Kettle and the other chiefs rode into camp from just returning from Denver and the Camp Weld Council, he heard that it was Evans who put the negotiations in the hands of Colonel Chivington. He writes that the chiefs remained puzzled by what Chivington had said and could not make out clearly what his intentions were. "The truth probably was that he had already laid his plans for the attack on our camp, which he carried out with such terrible effect a few weeks later; so in his talk he said nothing to alarm the chiefs or to disturb their belief that peace was soon to be concluded," and added that based on what Bent was told was, that he (Chivington) was careful, however to make no promises.[14]

***

Letter Eighteen
to Col. John Chivington

October 11th, 1864
Fort Lyon, Colorado Territory

Colonel

I arrived with Major Wynkoop on saturday [sic]. The command has not arrived yet but we expect them today. There is no news of importance here. There are about two hundred Indians camped fifteen miles from here awaiting the return of the chiefs. Left Hand is here with about twenty Indians. Today he says if all the rest go to war he will with his band lay down their arms and come in for protection, or fight even against his own tribe rather than take up arms against the whites. I suppose you have heard of the trouble Capt. Butcher

---
14. Hyde, 146.

had with Co. G during our absence. He declared the Co in mutiny and called out the Garrison. My Company was the only one, he informs me, that obeyed orders and came to his support. G. Company was put in the Guard house and set fire to it that night. It Joined the magazine and it was a wonder that the whole post was not blown up. All the ammunition at this Post was stored in that building amounting to several tons. Major Wynkoop has today set Co. G. to work building a new Guard House.

I am anxious to hear from Denver hoping to receive orders to return. My Company should be mustered out this month but the Major says he cannot spare us from the Post although there are only eight or ten here to be mustered out and there is one full Company of New Mexican troops here besides our two Cos.

Major Wynkoop sent Lieut Dennison by yesterday's Coach with dispatches to Generals Curtis and Blunt with particulars in regard to our Indian affairs asking what course to pursue. Lieut Phillips is Post Adjutant. I am the only officer with my Company and if there is no Lieut assigned to me I would like to have Lieut Olney or any one in prefferense [sic] to Leonard. I would also like to have Phillips retained as 1st Lieut. You know that I am not much of a scribe and would like to have a good business Lieutenant as I shall of necessity be absent sometimes from my Company. And such a man as Lenard [sic], who can scarcely write his name is not the kind of man I would like to have in charge of my Company and property. You told me that our Regament [sic] would retain its organization. If so, we will have to recruit. I think I can raise about two hundred out of the hundred day Reg as soon as their time is out, if you should think proper to have me detailed for that service. If I am not ordered by Denver to the next mail,

Colonel, you would confer a favor on me by writing a few lines in answer to this. I am very desirous to get my business affairs with the Q. Master, Ordinance and your office settled as soon as possible as I wish to make application about next February for a furlough to go to Maine to see my Mother and Sisters. I have not been across the Mo. River but once in ten years and have not seen my folks for five. Any thing I can do for you officially or unofficially I shall always be pleased to do.

Yours respectfully

Silas S. Soule

-Raymond G. Carey Collection
Special Collections
University of Denver

***

"I'm not much of a scribe." This short sentence made me stop in my tracks. As we have seen in his letters he loves to write. He's thoughtful, sometimes eloquent, frequently humorous, explains daily life and travel with the greatest of details. While this letter helps explain life at the fort, it also serves as an omen for what is coming in the near future, the question of recruiting, and why is recruiting back in the conversation.

This is a letter that is not found in Silas' military records and correspondence at the National Archives. For the longest time it was a complete mystery to me how Dr. Raymond Carey discovered it. Dr. Gary L. Roberts was the first scholar allowed to go through the Dr. Raymond Carey Collection at the University of Denver after his death and in an interesting twist of fate, Roberts suspects that Dr. Carey discovered this letter in the records of the Military District of Colorado records in the National Archives. In this letter, says Roberts, "He's still loyal."[15] But not for much longer.

This letter is full of the details of daily fort life but is in some ways full of mysterious intersections. To begin with, Chief Left Hand, a Southern Arapaho chief, is working tirelessly for peace at Fort Lyon. He has followed the direction of moving closer to the fort, and he and Silas seem to have made a connection around the talk of peace.

Silas reports of a mutiny, a fire in the guard house, and the threat of all the ammunition blowing up, all of which seems incredibly out of character at Fort Lyon. He says the Major can't do without him for mustering out his papers, but he doesn't officially make a request to Ned for another five days, which is denied. Lt. Dennison travels to Fort Riley to get "the particulars in regard to our Indian affairs asking what course to pursue," which is the plan for peace that Ned has crafted.

There seems some strong feelings about who will be Silas' scribe in the day-to-day workings at the fort, and he is quite particular about who he wants, and who he doesn't want, and then he confronts Chivington with the claim that "You told me that our Regament [sic] would retain its organization. If so, we will have to recruit. I think I can raise about two hundred out of the hundred day Reg as soon as their time is out, if you should think proper to have me detailed for that." In a quirky twist of timing, he wants to go back to recruiting, and he believes he can recruit 200 out of the 100-Dayers to sustain the Regiment. These are the 100-Dayers who are the inexperienced, poorly trained soldiers who will be the perpetrators of horrific violence at the Sand Creek Massacre five weeks later after this letter is written. I can't help but think back to Park Ranger Byron Parker at the Battle of Glorietta battlefield site in Pecos, NM, asking me months earlier, with maps unrolled and sprawled around tables at the visitor's

---

15. Gary Roberts, phone interview, December 6, 2024.

center for my interview, asking "what is he recruiting for?"

Towards the end, as if maybe this is the real reason for this letter, he makes the pitch that he needs to settle his business affairs "as I wish to make application about next February for a furlough to go to Maine to see my Mother and Sisters. I have not been across the Mo. River but once in ten years and have not seen my folks for five." This longing to get home in so many letters we have read over the years is becoming heartbreaking to me. He can't get home and wants desperately to be home. He pleads his case by adding up the years he's been gone, as if these numbers should be enough for a furlough request to be approved. And they should be.

The tone of this letter is strangely different than others, filled with the details of the fort that would not necessarily be the news of the day required by Chivington. However, it's this letter that he writes to Chivington that begins with "there are about two hundred Indians camped fifteen miles from here awaiting the return of the chiefs" that challenges historian Gary L. Roberts. Roberts believes that what Silas has unwittingly done is that he has tipped off Chivington that the Cheyenne and Arapaho are in close proximity to the fort. "Silas has helped reveal the location. I wonder what the imprint was on Silas as he reflected [on writing this letter]" and asked himself, "why did I write that letter?"[16]

Wynkoop has told the Cheyenne and Arapaho chiefs to bring their tribes to the fort and camp near the post and they begin gathering with the beginning of Chief Left Hand's arrival. In his testimony, Silas said that Ned told the chiefs that he would immediately send to General Curtis and see if peace could not be made, and sent Lt. Dennison to Fort Riley, Kansas Territory, which we read in this letter. And so, begins the arrival of the Cheyenne and Arapaho coming in, complying with Ned's orders, and begin camping near the post. Even-

---

16. Roberts, interview.

tually, he says in his testimony in the Congressional Inquiry, 106 lodges came into the post, "Arapahos and Cheyennes – mostly Arapaho."[17]

"I think they remained at the post about two weeks, until Major Scott Anthony came from Denver and relieved Major Wynkoop from command at Fort Lyon. Major Anthony told the Indians that they must give up their arms, and horses and mules which belonged to the government or to the whites. This he told to Little Raven (Arapaho chief), then in command of the village near the post. Little Raven gave up three rifles, one pistol, and I think about sixty bows and quivers; nine horses and mules." [18]

No messenger ever arrives at Fort Lyon with word from General Curtis.

***

I've bundled the following two letters, to Wynkoop and Chivington, together to examine the timing, the rejection, and the mystery of no response. Silas does not get permission to go to Denver to sort through his papers to muster his men out. According to his military records he is at Fort Lyon the entire month of October.

Letter Nineteen
to Major E. W. Wynkoop (Ned)

October 16th, 1864
Fort Lyon, Colorado Territory

---

17. Silas Soule Testimony, 9.
18. Ibid.

Major

I have the honor to report for your consideration that the term of service of my Co. D. 1st Cavalry of Col expires on the 31st of this month and most of the men to be mustered out are at Denver City C.T. where they were mustered into service and have no descriptive Rolls with them. Consequently, cannot be mustered out without my presence. Therefore I would most respectfully ask that I be ordered to Denver so that I may make out the necessary papers and verify the presence of the men to be mustered out in complyance [sic] with circular G6 War Department dated May 1864.

I am sir with much respect

Your obt servant
Silas S. Soule
Capt 1st Cav of Col
Comdy [Commanding] Co D.

To Major E. Wynkoop
1st Cav of Colorado
Comdy [Commanding] Fort Lyon C.T.

[On the back side of this letter, is the following]
Fort Lyon, CT

October 16th /64

Respectfully returned to 1st Lt Soule with the information that if I sent the commanding officer of each Company to Denver with few men they have to be mustered out. It would leave me without any Company officers at this Garrison and I cannot see why the Commanding Officer of each Company cannot make out the necessary papers here at the HeadQuarters of his Company if he cannot at make out those papers he is alone to become.

E. Wynkoop
Major - 1st Calvary
Comdg. Ft Lyon

-Miliary Records, National Archives

***

Letter Twenty
to Col. John Chivington

October 17th, 1864
Fort Lyon, Colorado Territory

Colonel J.M. Chivington
Comdg [Commanding] Dist of Col

Sir

I have made application to Major Wynkoop to order me to Denver to have my Company mustered out as they have not the necessary papers with them and I cannot make them out here as I have left some of my papers in Denver which I expected by the last mail but failed to receive. I have [need] them and am in [hopes] I will receive them by the next mail. If I do not my men cannot be mustered out and if I do it is doubtful whether they will be mustered without my presence. If I receive orders to go to Denver by return mail I could get there in time. The Major refuses to let me go and I will not have time to receive an answer from Genl Blunt were I to make an application. Therefore if it is possible for you to have orders for me I would like much to receive them by return mail.

I am with much respect

Your obt servant
Silas S. Soule
Capt 1st Cav of Col

-Military Records, National Archives

***

Silas asks Wynkoop, and Ned says no. He writes to Chivington, and we don't know what he said in return, but he doesn't get permission. And yet Silas, is already thinking of "making application" to General Blunt. This is a highly unusual response for Silas, who we have observed now for almost three years in military service, has followed the hierarchy of the military. Questions frequently, for sure, but has not gone above Ned like this in any other military correspondence.

We don't know why he doesn't get what he wants. Maybe the papers do come in the next mail (most likely not, because in the next letter to his sister, Annie, he still hopes to go to Denver to "fix up some papers"), but maybe some of the mystery can be revealed by looking at what is happening at Fort Lyon in October.

As mentioned in the previous essay, we read of Silas' understanding of Wynkoop's invitation to the Cheyenne and Arapaho to gather close to the fort. Here, George Bent also writes that Wynkoop had reassured the chiefs, telling them that it was all right and that they might bring their bands in near the fort and camp there until an answer to their peace proposals was received, so the Cheyenne broke camp on the Smoky Hill and moved down to Sand Creek, about forty miles northeast of Fort Lyon.[19]

By mid-October when Silas writes these letters, there are about 750 Cheyenne and Arapaho who have started assembling at Sand Creek, and it becomes a chief's village, with 33 chiefs and headman of Cheyenne and Arapaho present.[20]

Silas is aware of all the promises that have been made. The assurances that have been given. The workings of what peace looks like on the plains, from Smoky Hill to Sand Creek, are beginning to take flight.

It looks like there is hope in air as the fall winds blow in on southeastern Colorado.

***

Letter Twenty-One
to his sister, Annie

October 30th, 1864
Fort Lyon, Colorado Territory

Dear Annie,

I received two letters from you by last mail. One I think came around by way of California as it was dated Sep 7th. I am still at Fort Lyon. Have been to Denver once since I came down here but only stopped a week. I expect to be ordered up there soon to fix up some papers. If I do I shall endeavor to get a furlough to go to Maine. I want to see you and the rest of the folks. I suppose I shall continue in the service for three years

---

19. Hyde, 146.
20. Sand Creek Timeline, National Park Service.

more, don't know. I have not heard from Will since he left Lawrence. I have not written to him for the reason that I did not know where to direct.

We have had considerable trouble with the Indians this summer, but they are quite peaceable at present. There are about three thousand here within a mile of the post who have come in for the purpose of making peace. I do not know what we shall do but I think [the] government will not make peace with them. If that is the case we shall have some fighting to do this winter.

I am not in a very good humor to write this evening for the wind blows and it is cold and I can hardly see the lines on the paper. I received Miss Martingale's letter. I think she is a genious [sic] – would like to get acquainted with her. I received a letter from Hannah and answered it last week, also one from Em. Tell Mother that if I go back on a visit this winter, I am afraid I will not be able to send any money, but if I find that I cannot go I will send her some sure. Give my regards to all the folks in Bath, including the school marms. I received some papers by last mail which were very acceptable. There are a good many Maine folks here, mostly from the neighborhood of Bangor. I don't know of anything more to write and I am afraid you can't read this. If you can't, I will interpret when I go back. Do you ever hear from Glass' folks or Elsworths? Do you know whether Charley Coombs is in the Army now? Write me all that you can think of interest in your next.

Yours &c

Sile

-Anne E. Hemphill Collection

***

This letter illustrates what peace might be physically looking like in his life at Fort Lyon. Promises of safety that have been made, and also providing food, inviting the Cheyenne and Arapaho to camp near the fort. These are signs of welcome, hospitality and kindness as promises of peace. Peace has become the word. Promises of peace. Peace as food. Peace as place. Peace as kindness. Peace as welcoming. Peace as permission.

It's the end of October now and almost three months since the recruitment of the 100-Day Volunteers by Evans began. One month since returning from Denver and the Camp Weld Council. The landscape near Fort Lyon is changing with the arrival of thousands of Cheyenne and Arapaho, who have been invited to camp close by. Promises have been made. Integrity is on the line. Hope is present, until suddenly, it's not.

"Major Wynkoop had reassured the chiefs, telling them that it was all right and that they might bring their bands in near the fort and camp there until an answer to their peace proposals was received, wrote Bent, so the Cheyenne broke camp on the Smoky Hill and moved down to Sand Creek, about forty miles northeast of Fort Lyon. From this new camp the Cheyenne went in and visited Major Wynkoop and the people at the fort seemed so friendly that after a short time the Arapahos left us and moved right down to the fort, where they went into camp and received regular rations."[21]

Silas writes there are now 3,000 Cheyenne and Arapahos at Fort Lyon "for the purpose of making peace" and already suspects that the "Government will not make peace with them."

---

21. Hyde, 146.

He adds, "If that is the case, we shall have some fighting to do this winter." He knows the promises that have been made and is already suspicious that these promises will not be honored and be broken.

What nobody sees coming next is that Ned is removed from command at Fort Lyon, two weeks after this letter is written, which ultimately becomes devastating for those who are gathered outside the fort, and inside as well. He is relieved from command and reassigned to Fort Riley and Major Scott Anthony arrives to take command of the fort. Anthony is briefed on what agreements have been made, and what promises have been promised. This event, the why of reassigning Ned, becomes horrifically clear later in November. Some historians conclude that his reassignment is because he has made overtures of peace on his own, rather than through the military command. He went to Smoky Hill on his own. He escorts the Cheyenne and Arapaho chiefs to Denver to meet with Evans and Chivington at Camp Weld, without going through the proper channels. His reassignment is retribution.

Silas' papers didn't get sorted out. He doesn't get a furlough to Maine in the winter. His sister, Emily, lives in Bangor. His mom Sophia had several brothers and sisters living in Maine, so Silas has cousins, aunts, uncles and his sister who he hasn't seen in some time. He hasn't been back to Kansas since 1860. He's missing his family, quite desperately right now. He laments not knowing where Will is. We don't know if he gets the answers from Annie to where his friends are. This is the last letter to Annie in the collection.

The underpinning is that what has been routine and normal fort life, has become neither routine nor normal at the end of October 1864.

***

Letter Twenty-Two
to Major Scott J. Anthony, Commanding Post

Nov 25th, 1864
Fort Lyons, Colorado Territory

Sir.

I have the honor to request of the General commanding the Department of Kansas leave of absence for thirty Days with permission to apply for an extension. I have been an Officer in the service of the United States for the last three years and have not been off duty or had leave of absence during that time.

I have the honor to be the Most Respectfully Your Obt. Servt.

Silas S. Soule
Capt 1st Cav of Col
To Major Scott J. Anthony Comdg Post

-Correspondence contributed by Byron Strom
Published by the Soule Kindred, Vol IV, No 3 July 1970, 2

***

At the end of November 1864, there is so much we don't know about what motivates Silas to request a leave of absence on this day, except we know how desperate he is for a way back to Kansas. Ned has just been reassigned, and he leaves on the day Silas writes this request. Christmas is a month away.

A year earlier, President Abraham Lincoln had proclaimed Thanksgiving Day, the last Thursday of November, and in 1864, that day fell on November 24, the day before Silas wrote his request for a leave of absence.

Major Anthony immediately approves the request for leave and it's sent on its way to Fort Riley.

Two days after Silas requests this leave of absence, he gets the shock of his life, as he literally runs into Chivington and the 100-Day Volunteers who have been recruited by Evans, outside of Fort Lyon. He explained this unexpected shock with, "on the evening of the 27th [November], Lieutenant Minton and myself discovered some horsemen about fifteen miles above Fort Lyon; supposed them to be Indians. We returned to the fort and reported to Major Anthony. Major Anthony ordered me to take twenty men and go after them, supposing them to be hostile Indians. I proceeded up the Arkansas and about sunrise I met a mule team; inquired if there were Indians ahead and the driver told me that Colonel Chivington had ten or twelve companies (the asterisk here in the testimony identifies the companies as the Third regiment, Colorado cavalry, one-hundred-days men) of "one hundred-dayers. On, about two miles further, I went and met Colonel Chivington and about, I suppose, one thousand men (soldiers). Colonel Chivington asked me if they knew he was coming at Fort Lyon. I told him they did not, and that I had learned from the person with the mule team, two miles below, that he was coming. Colonel Chivington then rode ahead of the command to Fort Lyons. I remained and came in with the third regiment, or a little ahead of them."[22]

There still has been no word from General Curtis about the peace plan.

---

22. Silas Soule Testimony, 10.

Chivington arrives literally in the dark of night at the door of Fort Lyon within days following the transfer of power from Wynkoop to Anthony. In fact, in his testimony, Silas was asked if Chivington asked him if there were Arapahos and Cheyenne still at the fort on the night of November 27. He answered, "I said that there were some Indians camped near the fort, below the fort, but they were not dangerous; that they were waiting to hear from General Curtis."[23] Silas described Chivington's arrival as "having moved so secretly that we were not aware of their approach."

The next day, November 28, "Captain William Bent and John Vogle were arrested and guards placed around their houses. They then declared their intention to massacre the friendly Indians camped on Sand Creek. As soon as I knew of their movement I was indignant as you would have been were you here and went to Cannon's room, where a number of officers of the 1st and 3rd were congregated and told them that any man who would take part in the murders, knowing the circumstances as we did, was a low lived, cowardly son of a bitch." He was threatened. Military colleagues Captain Johnson and Lt. Harding went to camp and reported Silas to Chivington, Downing and the "whole outfit what I had said, and you can bet hell was to pay in camp. Chiv and all hands swore they would hang me before they moved camp, but I stuck it out, and all the officers at the Post, except Anthony backed me."

And then, "I was then ordered with my whole company to Major A– with 20 days rations. I told him I would not take part in their intended murder, but if they were going after the Sioux, Kiowa's or any fighting Indians, I would go as far as any of them. They said that was what they were going for, and I joined them."

***

---

23. Ibid.

Letter Twenty-Three
to his friend, Major Edward Wynkoop

December 14th, 1864
Fort Lyon, Colorado Territory

Dear Ned:

Two days after you left here the 3rd Reg. with a Battalion of the 1st arrived here, having moved so secretly that we were not aware of their approach until they had Pickets around the Post, allowing no one to pass out! They arrested Capt. Bent and John Vogle, and placed guards around their houses. They then declared their intention to massacre the friendly Indians camped on Sand Creek. Major Anthony gave all information, and eagerly Joined in with Chivington & Co, and ordered Lieut. Cramer, with is whole Co to Join the command. As soon as I knew of their movement I was indignant as you would have been were you here, and went to Cannon's room, where a number of officers of the 1st and 3rd were congregated and told them that any man who would take part in the murders, knowing the circumstances as we did, was a low lived cowardly son of a bitch. Capt J.J. Johnson and Lieut. Harding went to camp and reported to Chiv, Downing and the whole outfit what I had said, and you can bet hell was to pay in camp.

Chiv and all hands swore they would hang me before they moved camp, but I stuck it out, and all the officers at the Post, except Anthony backed me. I was then ordered with my whole company to Major A– with 20 days rations. I told him I would not take part in their intended murder, but if they were going after the Sioux, Kiowa's or any fighting Indians, I would go as far as any of them. They said that was what they were going for, and I joined them.

We arrived at Black Kettle and Left Hand's Camp at day light. Lieut. Wilson and Co.'s "C," "E" & "G" were ordered in advance to cut off their herd. He made a circle to the rear and formed a line 200 yds from the village, and opened fire. Poor Old John Smith and Louderbeck ran out with white flags but they paid no attention to them, and they ran back to their tents. Anthony then rushed up with Co's "D" "K" & "G," to within one hundred yards and commenced firing. I refused to fire and swore that none but a coward would for by this time hundreds of women and children were coming toward us and getting on their knees for mercy. Anthony shouted, "kill the sons of bitches" Smith and Louderbeck came to our command, although I am confident there were 200 shots fired at them. For I heard an officer say that Old Smith and any one who sympathized with the Indians, ought to be killed and now was a good time to do it. The Battery then came up in our rear, and opened on them. I took my comp'y across the Creek, and by this time the whole of the 3rd and the Batteries were firing into them and you can form some idea of the slaughter. When the Indians found there was no hope for them they went for the Creek and got under the banks and some of the Bucks got their bows and a few rifles and defended themselves as well as they could. By this time there was no organization among our troops, they were a perfect mob – every man on his own hook. My Co. was the only one that kept their formation, and we did not fire a shot.

The massacre lasted six or eight hours, and a good many Indians escaped. I tell you Ned it was hard to see little children on their knees have their brains beat out by men professing to be civilized. One squaw was wounded and a fellow took a hatchet to finish her, she held her arms up to defend her, and he cut one arm off and held the other with one hand and dashed the hatchet through her brain. One squaw with her two children were on their knees, begging for their lives of a dozen soldiers, within ten feet of them all, firing – when one succeeded in hitting the squaw in the thigh, when she took a knife and cut the throats of both children and then killed herself. One old Squaw hung herself in the lodge – there was not enough room for her to hang and she held up her knees and choked herself to death. Some tried to escape on the Prairie, but most of them were run down by horsemen. I saw two Indians hold one of another's hands, chased until they were exhausted, when they kneeled down, and clasped each other around the neck and both were shot together. They were all scalped, and as high as half a dozen taken from one head. They were all horribly mutilated. One woman was cut open and a child taken out of her, and scalped.

White Antelope, War Bonnet, and a number of others had Ears and Privates cut off. Squaws snatches were cut out for trophies. You would think it impossible for white men to butcher and mutilate human beings as they did there, but every word I have told you is the truth, which they do not deny. It was almost impossible to save any of them. Charly Autobee save John Smith and Winsers squaw. I saved little Charlie Bent. Geo. Bent was killed. [George Bent was wounded but survived.] Jack Smith was taken prisoner, and murdered the next day in his tent by one of Dunn's Co. "E". I understand the man received a horse for doing the job. They were going to murder Charlie Bent, but I run him into the Fort. They were going to kill Old Uncle John Smith, but Lt. Cannon and the boys of Ft.

Lyon, interfered, and saved him. They would have murdered Old Bents family, if Col. Tappan had not taken the matter in hand. Cramer went up with twenty (20) men, and they did not like to buck against so many of the 1st. Chivington has gone to Washington to be made General, I suppose, and get authority to raise a nine months Reg't to hunt Indians. He said Downing will have me cashiered if possible. If they do I want you to help me. I think they will try the same for Cramer for he has shot his mouth off a good deal, and did not shoot his pistol off in the Massacre. Joe has behaved first rate during this whole affair. Chivington reports five or six hundred killed, but there were not more than two hundred, about 140 women and children and 60 Bucks. A good many were out hunting buffalo. Our best Indians were killed. Black Kettle, One Eye, Minnemic, and Left Hand. [Black Kettle was not killed.] Geo. Pierce of Co. "F" was killed trying to save John Smith. There was one other of the 1st killed and nine of the 3rd all through their own fault. They would get up to the edge of the bank and look over, to get a shot at an Indian under them. When the women were killed the Bucks did not seem to try and get away, but fought desperately. Charly Autobee wished me to write all about it to you. He says he would have given anything if you could have been there.

I suppose Cramer has written to you, all the particulars, so I will write half. Your family is well. Billy Wilker, Col. Tappen, Wilson (who was wounded in the arm) start for Denver in the morning. There is not news I can think of. I expect we will have a hell of a time with Indians this winter. We have (200) men at the Post – Anthony in command. I think he will be dismissed when the facts are known in Washington. Give my regards to any friends you come across, and write as soon as possible.

Yours, SS

(signed) S.S. Soule

-Colorado Historical Society Collection

***

There are many benches at the Sand Creek Massacre National Historic Site to sit down on and breathe while taking in the landscape and the words of this letter. There is a wonderful bench at the Repatriation Site designed by Descendants, located just at the beginning of the Bluff Trail. The bench overlooks the unmarked sacred ground where human remains have been returned to the land. Deep breaths. And more deep breaths. A sweet breeze reminds me to leave this bench, to continue on the trail that parallels the Massacre site for a while, and read another sign that speaks of violence, in the quiet valley where the Big Sandy sits today.

I've listened to Sand Creek Massacre Descendant Otto Braided Hair speak of Silas for more than 20 years. I hear reverence every time. Gratitude every time. Otto is Northern Cheyenne and has been the caretaker and original organizer for the annual Spiritual Healing Run that begins around the anniversary at the Massacre site each fall, usually around the anniversary date, November 29. Cheyenne and Arapaho runners' rendezvous from Oklahoma, Wyoming and Montana at the site, run to Eads, then up the back roads, following the trail the soldiers took back to Denver. This Spiritual Healing Run has become a source of healing, of remembrance.

When the runners get to Denver, the next morning the run continues at Riverside Cemetery at Silas' grave. The people gathered are offered the smoke of cedar and sweetgrass as a blessing. The 33-star flag, like the one Black Kettle raised in those first few moments at sunrise, along with the white flag, are raised at the flagpole in the Grand Army of the Republic graves, just a few steps from Silas' grave. The drummers sing a Veteran's Song, and a Flag Raising Song. This letter is read by Silas's descendant Byron Strom at the invitation of Otto. For the young, first-time runners, this is the first time they have heard these words spoken, this letter read out loud, the horrific violence on their relatives by those 100-Dayers commanded by the Methodist minister and orchestrated with the Methodist governor of the Colorado Territory. Some years the sky overhead at the cemetery ceremony is robin egg blue; some years there is fresh snow on the ground, and some years the fog moves in, the sky is grey, and no one can see the beloved Rocky Mountains above even the tallest cemetery gravestones. It's somber. Some years honking geese have flown over, but it's a sacred quiet time to take it all in, the burning cedar and sweetgrass, the drums, the singing, the storytelling.

Otto is the last of his generation to tell the story of the Sand Creek Massacre, and the day his great-grandfather Braided Hair woke to the sound of what he thought was buffalo hoofs, and instead were the soldier's horses. His great-grandfather put his pregnant great-grandmother on a horse, and she got away. She was found near frozen on the horse and had to be pried off. She survived, and so did Otto's great-grandfather. He says telling the story of what happened at Sand Creek is "a commitment handed down in the generations. I carry on as long as I can."[24]

The first time I heard this letter read out loud was in 2003 when Byron read it for the first time at Silas' grave at the first Spiritual Healing Run that convened at Silas' grave. There is something so meaning making when someone reads a

---

24. Otto Braided Hair interview, Faith Talks: In Remembrance of the Sand Creek Massacre, United Women in Faith: Faith Talks, United Methodist Church, November 25, 2024.

letter out loud, but more profound when it speaks of such horrific violence. It shatters the human spirit that a group of Colorado soldiers could do these acts of violence. I'm sure I winced many times hearing the words echo from one horrible unspeakable act spoken out loud, to the next, and to the next.

"I remember being pretty uncomfortable," Byron said recently.[25] He had been invited to the 2003 ceremony at Riverside by his friend Vonnie Perkins and had brought the letter with him. On the spur of the moment Otto asked him to read the letter in front of the large crowd gathered at the grave and the flagpole. "I came not prepared to do that." His dad, Malcolm, who had long ago introduced the letters to Dr. Raymond Carey, who then shared them with the Denver Public Library and Colorado Historical Society so that I would discover them four years later, was there with us on that crisp and cold November morning in 2003.

After he read the letter, "I sat down and the women and the girls came up and gave me a hug. That still makes me emotional when I think about it." In October 2024 at the sacred gathering, he apologized for reading the letter but added "I will read this letter."

"It's meaning provides a connection between me and the Indian people. A connection between Silas and them because I'm connected to Silas." He read the letter again in 2008 at the first internment at the Repatriation Site of human remains at the Massacre site, and his dad was there as well.

Byron grew up knowing about Silas and these letters from his childhood. His mom, Edith, first spoke of them. It wasn't until he was in his 30s that he spoke to his Aunt Anne (his mom's sister and the family historian and preservationist of the letters) and said, "I need to know more than I know."

---

25. Byron Strom, phone interview with author, December 9, 2024.

Four generations after Silas' death, this family is now passing the collection of letters and stories, to another generation of Byron's daughters, and preparing the sixth generation of Byron's grandchildren.

The story of relatives connected through these letters is vast and wide, much like the land in southeastern Colorado today when one stands at the Repatriation Site. Connected through storytelling across generations of Cheyenne, Arapaho, and white people of European descent, it connects us all in the humanity of suffering, healing and reconciliation, every time they are read out loud.

Lastly, this letter made its way up the hierarchy of the military in December 1864 because of Ned. Ned took this letter up the ranks that ultimately forced the Congressional Inquiry in February 1865, and he is usually overlooked in the discussions about this letter, ensuring that it went where it needed to go. A word of gratitude to Ned, his moral compass and his repair work of trying to right a wrong. His commitment to the work of justice in sending this letter forth, combined with the profound and sacred oral history of the Cheyenne and Arapaho, have been the ways the world knows of the horrific atrocities of that day.

***

Letter Twenty-Four
to his mother, Sophia

December 18th, 1864
Fort Lyon, Colorado Territory

Dear Mother

I received a letter from you tonight and you bet I was glad to hear from you. I ought to write oftener, but I am so lazy and have so little that would interest you that I neglect to write. I wrote to Annie and sent the letter by Mr. Gould who belongs in Brunswick I believe. He has served three years in my Regament [sic] – is going to Bath – you will see him and he will tell you everything you want to know. I have not received any letter from Will since he left Lawrence. I think I will write to him in the morning although I don't believe he will receive it – the mails are so irregular. I receive letters from Annie and Em quite often and endeavor to answer them as soon as possible. I still have hopes of going to Maine this winter but may not until spring.

We have had considerable trouble with Indians this fall. The day you wrote I was present at a Massacre of three hundred Indians mostly women and children. It was a horrable [sic] scene and I would not let my Company fire. They were friendly and some of our soldiers were in their Camp at the time trading. It looked too hard for me to see little Children on their knees begging for their lives, have their brains beat out like dogs. It was a Regament [sic] of 100 days men who accomplished the noble deed. Some of the Indians fought when they saw no chance of escape and killed twelve and wounded forty of our men. I had one Horse shot. I have been an Indian scout for the last three weeks but don't think will have much more at present.

Tell Annie and Em that I am just beginning to receive papers from them for which I am very grateful [sic]. Give my love to every body and tell them that I would be glad to hear from them. I do not write near as often as I used to for I have so much to do to keep my Co papers correct. I am responsable [sic] for fifty thousand dollars worth of Government property which must be attended to. I will write occasionally. Don't get worried for there is not the least danger in the world of my getting killed, and as I am the most interested party, you should not fret. I believe I will write a letter to Uncle Ben. Good night.

Your Sonny

Sile

-Anne E. Hemphill Collection

***

"I was present at a Massacre." Imagine writing to your mother with this horrific news. He wants her to know some of the details but not know everything. He protects her in this letter from knowing it all, which is such a testimony about the kind of son she has. This last letter in 1864 ends with "don't get worried for there is not the least danger in the world of my getting killed."

Three weeks after the Massacre, Silas wrote this letter to his mother. Imagine for a moment that you are the relative he writes to, with the details of what happened. She is unaware that he crossed the Big Sandy multiple times over the course of hours during the Massacre with Colorado soldiers around him shooting and killing.

She is unaware that Ned returns to Fort Lyon just days after Silas wrote this letter, and "visited the field of slaughter which was still covered with the ghastly remains of the victims, three-fourths of them were women and children, among whom were many young infants, there was not a single body but what had been scalped, while many both male and female had been mutilated in such a manner that decency will not permit to be recorded here."[26]

---

26. Edward W. Wynkoop, edited with an introduction biography by Christopher B. Gerboth, *The Tall Chief, The Autobiography of Edward W. Wyn-*

She is unaware, and so is Silas, that human remains taken from those murdered by the soldiers, are brought to Denver as trophies and displayed in a theatre.

She is unaware, and so is Silas, that he will never return to Maine, this winter, or next spring. But he continued to live in hope that he would.

She is unaware of the horrific violence that he saw perpetrated by fellow soldiers. In his way, this letter may be a path to help us understand the human suffering of veterans in war in the 19th century. Something went morally wrong at the Big Sandy that day in the ways of war. While Silas' moral compass was pointed in the direction of disobeying orders, bearing witness, writing a letter, and let's not forget that he and Lt. Joseph Cramer, were only two out of 600 soldiers who disobeyed orders to engage. The price to pay of being a witness, is that he watched horrific violence come to innocent elders, women and children and witnessed the mutilation of those human bodies by those same soldiers.

During the attack, and throughout the following day, scalps and other body parts were cut from many of the victims. In addition, robes, headdresses, moccasins, and other personal items were taken from the bodies of the deceased. In the following years and generations, a portion of these items were donated, bequeathed, sold, or by other means, acquired by museums and other repositories.[27]

Weeks after the Massacre in the ensuing Cheyenne raids as retaliation, George Bent recalled that a "war party of young Cheyenne run across nine of Chivington's men who had taken

---

koop, 1856-1866, Monograph 9, 1993 (Denver, CO: Colorado Historical Society, 1995), 103.
27. Signage at Repatriation Site at the Sand Creek Massacre Site, December 8, 2024.

part in the Sand Creek affair and recently been discharged, as their term of service had expired and they were on their way east to the States. These men were all killed by the Cheyenne, and after the fight the Indians found in the valises two Indian scalps which were at once recognized as those of White Leaf and Little Wolf or Little Coyote (the son of Two Thighs). The scalps were easily identified, as one of them had hair unusually light in color, while the other scalp still had attached to it a peculiar little shell which Little Coyote had always worn on his scalplock. Little Bear and Touching Cloud, both still living, were with this war party, and they say when the Cheyennes recognized these scalps they were so enraged that they cut the bodies of the dead men all to pieces. They also found in these men's valises several other trophies from Sand Creek which the men were taking east to the States."[28]

I can't help but imagine the effects of the moral distress of watching his fellow soldiers mutilating human bodies had on Silas. He knew that promises of peace that had been assured. He watched those promises shatter with the violence he saw. He trusted his values, and moral compass, and never doubted disobeying orders, even when threatened. He didn't question what the right thing was to do, he knew what the right thing was to do.

Wrestling with this constellation of events from the twenty-first century – knowing what is right from wrong, disobeying orders, being threatened, witnessing horrific violence and mutilation, writing about it – speaks to me of Silas's great emotional need to get to his family in Kansas or in Maine, that is so clearly apparent now more than ever as we come to the end of 1864.

---

28. Hyde, 181.

Chapter Eight
The Last Letter, 1865

Written in the early weeks of the New Year, this letter describes some of the profound changes on the horizon that are coming, especially with Silas' mustering out of the military. The nation has been grieving four years with the American Civil War which comes to an end in April, and a nation is plunged into mourning, also in April with the assassination of President Abraham Lincoln. Sadly, the Soule family will also be mourning in April. This is the only letter written in 1865 in our collection.

Letter Twenty-Five
to his mother, Sophia

January 8th, 1865
Fort Lyon, Colorado Territory

Dear Mother

I suppose you are anxious to hear from me. I should have written oftener if I had not been so busy fixing up my papers. Our Reg has been mustered out, 3 years having expired, and all the officers are relieved from duty at this Post. And I amongst the rest want to get my papers all square so if I go out I can start for the states right off but the officers think that I will be retained in the Veterans organization. At any rate I can if I wish and I have been thinking the matter over and believe it is best. For if I go back I don't know of any thing I could do at that would pay for I am too lazy to work you well know. The only chance would be to marry a rich widow. Do you think there is a good chance in Maine or will I find richer ones out west? I had applied for a leave of absence to go to Maine and just received answer from it saying that our Regt was to be immediately reorganized so I will have to wait and may not see you before March.

I suppose you have seen Mr. Gould. I sent a letter by him. He will tell you all about killing Indians. I spent New Years day on the battle ground counting dead Indians. There were not as many killed as was reported. There was not more than 130 killed, but most of them were women and children and all of them scalped. I hope the authorities at Washington will investigate the killing of those Indians. I think they will be apt to hoist some of our officials. I would not fire on the Indians with my Co and the Col said he would have me cashiered but he is out of the service before me and I think I stand better than he does in regard to his great Indian fight.

I am reforming in regard to my bad habits, Mother, for I have left off chewing tobacco and smoking a pipe but I will smoke cigars when I can get them. I don't drink so you see I am getting quite respectable and will stand a chance of getting a wife when I go down east. I am going to write Will this evening. I have not written since he went south. I wish you a Merry Christmas and happy New year. Wish I could send you a present, but our Pay master died Christmas and we have had no pay for 4 months. I am almost broke.

Your affectionate Son

Sile

-Anne E. Hemphill Collection

***

"I spent New Year's day on the battle ground counting dead Indians." It's a new year. It's been more than a month since the Massacre. He longs to be home. His request for a leave of absence is denied as he is mustered out of service. He hopes to return home in March, always writing in hope that he will get home.

You may wonder why this is the only letter that was written in 1865. Based on all I know, especially of what is to come, Silas will experience much joy and sorrow in these first few months of the new year that most likely kept him from writing to his mother and sisters. Firstly, he is mustered out of services, so there are no longer any letters in his military records. He starts his new job as adjunct provost marshal in January. Second, the Congressional Testimony begins in February, and he is the first witness. He is on the witness stand in Denver from February 15-February 21 and in reading the testimony there are many difficult places where he recounts the events leading up to, and at the Sand Creek Massacre. Though we have no evidence that he wrote about his beloved Hersa Coberly in his letters, he marries her on April 1. His life is abundantly full in bittersweet ways, and it appears there is little time to share it with his family in letters. These first few months of 1865 are also the last few months of his life.

Those bodies that Silas counts on New Year's Day are remains that were left at the Massacre location and were still seen in the 1870s. William Tecumseh Sherman, arrived in 1867 and removed human remains and artifacts from the Massacre location that were laying on the land.[1] There are still remains there today, covered by decades of blowing land. Sand Creek Massacre Descendants have taken possession of human remains that have been repatriated, including hairs that were returned by Yale University from a scalp taken at the Massacre, and a descendant of a soldier at the Massacre returned human remains in 2007, said Regional Superintendent Eric Leonard.[2] The first repatriation of human remains from the Sand Creek Massacre was on June 2, 2008, with the anticipation that "additional remains and objects from the massacre will be interred here in the future."[3]

A sign at the Repatriation Site in three languages – Cheyenne, Arapaho, and English - describes this sacred land with these words, "many years have passed. The land is still here. We lived here, our clans lived here. The land here is our home – we have come back home."

"The stories of Sand Creek are family histories for descendants; it's like it happened yesterday, it has not diminished in 160 years. The Massacre site is a place of healing.."[4] Dr. Alexa Roberts, the first superintendent of the Sand Creek Massacre National Historical Site, describes the Massacre location as "a living space that lives through the Descendants every day."

In his letter, Silas' estimate of the number of Cheyenne and Arapaho killed at the Massacre is low (today the number of Cheyenne and Arapaho killed is 230 elders, women and chil-

---

1. Tim Job, interview, Sand Creek Massacre National Historic Site, October 26, 2024.
2. Eric Leonard, interview, LaJunta, CO, October 24, 2024.
3. Signage at repatriation site at the Sand Creek Massacre Site, December 8, 2024.
4. Alexa Roberts, phone interview, October 30, 2024.

dren) but imagine the honesty he is writing to his mother with the details of the violence he witnessed. It takes moral courage to be transparent with his mother about this aspect of witnessing what he saw. He really wants the world to know, and will not be silent, beginning with his mom.

Theologian and ethicist Dr. Rita Nakashima Brock describes passages in this letter, and the previous two, as his "repair work."[5] The senior vice president for moral injury recovery programs at Volunteers of America, Brock, who self-identifies as Japanese American, is a national expert on moral injury, which she says is a set of symptoms, and not a disease. "It's a way of how people figure out how to live in a way that doesn't collapse you. Moral injury is moral distress that wakes them up at night. Witnesses to horrific violence in the military, like Silas, can ask questions like 'why did I sign up for this,' or could be angry at God. We don't see these examples in Silas, but what we read is that he has a reaction to what he saw and is sharing his outrage.

"It would be weird to not have a reaction" to what he saw, says Brock. Moral outrage is a feeling of helplessness, she adds, "that you couldn't stop it," which is exactly what happened to Silas. He tried to stop the Sand Creek Massacre the night before and failed. "He knew what was going to happen was wrong, then not being able to stop it, because he failed to prevent it, is a sense of moral responsibility."

His determination to write these last three letters, says Brock, is that Silas was "willing to take a risk to make it [the Sand Creek Massacre] known," she said, as well as express "a sense of moral outrage." His comment in this letter, "I hope the authorities at Washington will investigate the killing of those Indians. I think they will be apt to hoist some of our officials," is a sign that he's trying to right that wrong." Brock also sees common aspects of Dietrich Bonhoeffer's struggle and Si-

---

5. Rita Nakashima Brock, phone interview, December 10, 2024.

las' struggle, especially connecting the elements of violence and pacifism in each of their stories, with moral conscience. "There is no choice."

Repair is a lifelong journey, she notes, and his "repair work" is found in these last letters to his mom, and his last letter to Ned. Writing these last three letters is how he tried to rebuild a moral life, said Brock.

I reached out to Brock because she is the expert on moral injury in our country today. Her willingness to be in conversation with Silas' letters, and sharing her perspective, was something that seemed so necessary to me in understanding what his moral injury was from trying to stop the Massacre from happening the night before, and from witnessing the horrific deaths and mutilation of Cheyenne and Arapaho people. Her perspective adds so much to the understanding of Silas, the trauma of knowing the promises of peace, and how he tried to right a wrong.

Her wisdom has been invaluable.

Chapter Nine
Racial Justice Pilgrimages with Silas

Rev. Bonnie Spencer knows a bit about racial justice pilgrimage.[1] She knows about bearing witness, ritual and ceremony, and about standing at a vigil. She's meandered to Israel to walk where Jesus walked. She was a pilgrim at Iona. She's been going on pilgrimages in her family history. She was part of the soil gathering ceremony at 14th and Larimer Streets in Denver and in Limon, CO, retrieving soil from the location of the Denver Jail in 1900 where Preston John Porter Jr., a Black 15-year old boy was held and beaten in November 1900, before being placed on a train to Limon, CO where he was lynched and burned to death after he arrived.[2] She and others from the Colorado Lynching Memorial Project brought the soil on a pilgrimage to Montgomery, AL in April 2024 to be placed in the soil collection at the Legacy Museum, where 800 other jars of soil collected from lynching sites across America are housed.[3]

Byron Strom (great-great nephew of Silas) knows about pilgrimages from his home to the Sand Creek Massacre site

---

1. Bonnie Spencer, interview, Denver, CO, November 1, 2024.
2. Historical marker in Denver Memorializes Racial Terror Lynching of 15-Year-Old Boy, Equal Justice Initiative, November 28, 2020, https://eji.org/.
3. Equal Justice Initiative, accessed December 20, 2024, https://eji.org/.

where his ancestor Silas Soule disobeyed orders and watched the seven-hour Massacre unfold. So does Betty Nguyen, superintendent of nurturing leadership and belonging at Mountain-Sky Conference of the United Methodist Church who travels to Riverside Cemetery where every year a ceremony is hosted by the Cheyenne and Arapaho people at Silas' grave as part of the annual Spiritual Healing Run.

In this chapter, I hope that you find yourself thinking about being or becoming a pilgrim. Whether it be a day trip, an overnight, or a journey of a few days, how would your travels look different if you claimed yourself as one on a pilgrimage. In this chapter, may you discover new ways of carving out pilgrimages in your everyday life. Rita Bergland, who has traveled the world on pilgrimages, points us in one direction of claiming travel as pilgrimage. What would our travels be like if we framed them around pilgrimages and considered ourselves pilgrims of today.[4] What really is pilgrimage?

"It's not tourism," says Rita Bergland, a licensed professional counselor and leader of pilgrimages offered around the globe.[5] Bergland says the difference between tourism and pilgrimage is that 'we are going to be in relationship with people and with places where they are also going to enter into a relationship with us. I'm not going to go and look at an object, take a photo of it and take it home…It's a two-way relational experience. In doing so, I'm saying I'm here to be changed in this relationship. I'm here to be impacted and influenced in this relationship."

Rev. Spencer suggests that "tourism is observing things, that we stand at a distance. Pilgrimage asks, how am I changed?

---

4. In some circles, the word "pilgrim" is a heavy one, denoting the pilgrims who gathered with Indigenous peoples, and brought disease, and perpetuated genocide.
5. Rita Bergland, The Transformative Journey of Pilgrimage, The Allender Center, May 12, 2023, accessed on October 4, 2024, https://theallendercenter.org/2023/05/the-transformative-journey-of-pilgrimage/.

How can I make a difference?" Spencer's practice is to take a journal on a pilgrimage. She grounds her pilgrimages by setting intentions every day, which includes a morning prayer and an evening prayer. Like Bergland, Spencer believes that one must be open to being changed while on a pilgrimage.

Racial justice pilgrimages can bring people together to be intentionally connected to each other around doing racial justice work by witnessing places that are sacred, and usually painful. Or one can journey as an individual to places as a solo pilgrim, setting a daily schedule to pilgrim alone, and create destinations and moments to be opened to be changed or transformed.

Place can change us. Being at a place where change happened, like Selma, AL or the site of the Sand Creek Massacre, makes meaning. Experiencing these sites offer new possibilities of understanding, new transformation, new reconciliation, new hope, and possibly, new ways of healing. We can be changed by simply showing up and taking whatever it is, into our body, doing the head and heart work of justice seeking. For me, as a white, elder, cis-gender Protestant clergywoman of European descent, I am also healing by witnessing the history of racial injustice and holding myself accountable to it, inviting myself to grieve and lament it, moving forward into whatever healing is and looks like for oneself and our communities of accountability.

That's what I did during the fall of 2024. I wanted to visit as many places as I could where Silas wrote his letters. I went everywhere except Harrisburg, PA. I yearned to stand where he stood, like at Fort Garland. I wanted to travel on roads, or trails, that existed in 1862, from southern Colorado into New Mexico, across Raton Pass, and into Fort Union. I wanted to see the landscape that he saw on the road from Golden to Black Hawk on the Golden Gate Canyon Road.

And I wanted to be open to change, or surprise, or see something that was surprising, unplanned, or entirely unpredictable. I was stunned to discover that there was an internment camp in Santa Fe, NM where 4,000 American men of Japanese descent were imprisoned together during World War II, and the only public recognition of this history was on plaque on a rock in a dog park. I was equally surprised by a lone monument to Confederates located in central New Mexico, built in 1936 in the wave of monument installation by the United Daughters of the Confederacy. In both cases of monuments in public places, I was changed by stumbling along something new and equally disturbing that forced me to think in a new way around the historical American West.

So here are the pilgrimages I traveled for this book and I've thrown in one from a pilgrimage to Kansas during my doctoral work in 2022, for good measure. I set some intentions on my pilgrimages, and I invite you to do the same.

My first intention was silence in the car, which meant no music, radio, or podcasts. Those would be distractions that would take me out of the moment, and I really wanted to be in the moment wherever I was. Second, if something caught my curiosity, I would yield to it and stop. Turns out, this happened mostly around monuments and memorials, or surprise signage. My third intention was to always know where I was going to sleep that night. Traveling alone, I wanted my people at home to always know what route I was going to take to get to my final destination of the day. There were some unexpected mysteries to this intention in the San Luis Valley on my pilgrimage to Fort Garland and Conejos, but for the most part, I was spot on in having a good sense of distance, time, weather, and housing availability. My fourth intention was to never eat at a restaurant chain, and always choose local restaurants. I asked for recommendations of locals everywhere I went, and sometimes that was successful, sometimes not so much, but I always trusted it, in hopes that I would have the most wonderful meal, or coffee, or delicious donut, croissant, or fantastic slice of pie.

Finally, my last intention was to not be rushed. My deepest desire was to take in what is happening in the moment, and not to move on too quickly. Sometimes that looked like silence, sometimes a prayer, or sometimes a place to picnic and be nourished. As I look back on these pilgrimages now, I believe that this last intention was the greatest pilgrimage gift I created for myself.

New Mexico: Six Days and Five Nights

I left Denver early in the morning, knowing I had a reservation to stay in Santa Fe, NM that night. Denver is where Silas would have left with the First Regiment from Camp Weld to Fort Union, NM in 1862. I imagined at the time of this pilgrimage that he would have traveled in essence, the route I would take along I-25, seeing Long's Peak when he left, Pike's Peak in what is now Colorado Springs, seeing the Spanish Peaks outside of what is now Walsenburg, crossing over Raton Pass and then marching into Fort Union.

I was going further that first day to Santa Fe, but made a surprise stop at the memorial to the Ludlow Massacre, located a mile off the highway, between Walsenburg and Trinidad, after seeing the Massacre sign on the highway. I've driven past it a bazillion times, and never stopped, but that day I did because I was ready to be in the moment. The Ludlow Tent Colony Site is a National Historic Landmark, marking the location on April 20, 1914, where 21 people died, including miners, women and children, following the armed state militia shooting miners, and then later in the day burning the camp by setting fires to the tents.[6]

---

6. United Mine Workers of America signage at Ludlow Massacre site, September 18, 2024.

I started the pilgrimage with bearing witness to 1914 state violence.

After arriving in Santa Fe late in the afternoon, my first stop was at the Soldier's Monument, originally created to commemorate the New Mexico Campaign of 1862, located in the historic Santa Fe Plaza. I was not prepared to see that the obelisk was toppled but came to quickly realize with compassion that the toppling happened during the national protest around George Floyd's murder in 2020. I meandered over to the historic La Fonda Restaurant for a late lunch of chili rellenos and then was off to the hotel. Because of my interview schedule, the following day was a free day, and I drove up to the Manhattan Project National Historic Park and meandered around the limited interpretation there, including stops of well-known architecture for housing and offices. Back on the road to squeeze in a drive through Bandelier National Monument, I traveled to the "Santa Fe Internment Camp" highway sign, that I had passed earlier in the morning, with an arrow pointing right. I meandered through neighborhoods, mostly unsure if this was the path, and stumbled upon a dog park with no signage to help point me in the direction where I thought I needed to be. Eventually, I landed at an overlook and a monument that explained about New Mexico's only internment camp for Americans of Japanese descent in World War II. The bronze plaque includes, "this marker is placed here as a reminder that history is a valuable teacher only if we do not forget our past. The italicized is rubbed shiny to make it obvious. My last pilgrim stop for the day was to Petroglyph National Monument. As it was closing and I had just a few minutes to spare, it was easy to realize the vastness of the landscape with neighborhood petroglyphs telling the story of traveling people over time in the suburbs of Albuquerque. The day ended with a magnificent dinner of enchiladas, brisket style, Christmas (red and green chili sauces) at a restaurant recommended to me by a local with great taste for New Mexican food.

The morning started early to head south to Socorro, and even more south to Fort Craig, where Silas wrote a late spring letter in 1862 to Walt Whitman. Made from adobe and managed by the Bureau of Land Management, Fort Craig is slowly eroding back into the land from which it came from. Silas describes a swimming competition at the Rio Grande River, but today the river looks very different than it was during his stay. The battlefield of the Battle of Valverde, which Silas writes to Walt about, is located adjacent to Fort Craig and is owned by Armendaris Ranch, which is in turn owned by Ted Turner. No interpretation and no preservation at this battlefield, but one can get close enough to the river and the battlefield for a moment to take in what happened here in 1862. From the highway on the San Marciel exit, across the highway, I made the surprise discovery of the Confederate monument commemorating soldiers who died or went missing at the battle. That morning with the New Mexico clouds rolling high above that monument, I stood in wonder about how this monument that honors those who died got here, and why. I knew why, but I was reading Clint Smith's *How the Word Is Passed, A Reckoning With The History of Slavery Across America* and he answered this monument question for me that I needed to hear. "As of 2019, according to a report from the Southern Poverty Law Center, there were nearly two thousand Confederate monuments, place names and other symbols that remained in public places around the country, like this one where I stood."[7] Smith continues writing that the creation of these monuments was not a harmless commemoration or merely an attempt to remember fallen Americans. "The creation of any monument sends a message, whether intentional or not." This Confederate monument, created in 1936 was the beginning of "a new generation of white Southerners who had no memory of the war, had come of age, and the United Daughters of the Confederacy had raised enough

---

7. Clint Smith, *How the Word Is Passed* (New York, NY: Hachette Book Group), 143.

money to build memorials to these men. The goal in part was to teach the younger generations of white Southerners who these men had been and that the cause they had fought was an honorable one. But there is another reason, not wholly disconnected from the first. These monuments were also built in an effort to reinforce white supremacy at a time when Black communities were being terrorized and Black social and political mobility impeded." Question answered.

A final stop at the historic Albuquerque Plaza to see signage pointing to two mountain howitzers commemorating the 1862 New Mexico Campaign. I walked up, read the plaque, took a picture, then watched. Up until this moment of watching, I had realized that this spot is not a typical destination, and maybe because today, most visitors, maybe pilgrims, don't seem interested in the mechanics of monuments with cannon. But as I walked away, I saw a group of men who had been standing around, go up to the monument after I left, and read the plaque. How one decides to engage is also a discerning question for the pilgrim.

Up early to visit where the Battle of Peralta was fought, which if it hadn't been for the sign on the highway, I would have kept traveling west well into eastern New Mexico. Silas wrote to Walt that he had fought Confederates here in a fairly small battle engagement. Today, the battlefield stretches over a major east-west highway, with a Catholic church on one side and a vacant lot overgrown with trees and shrubs on the other. On my way to the battlefield, I stopped at the Los Lunas Museum of Heritage and Arts where worker Monica had put a few books aside for me to read, including *Distant Bugles, Distant Drums, The Union Response to the Confederate Invasion of New Mexico* by Flint Whitlock.[8] In the random, surprise, unpredictable way a pilgrim can find herself, I flipped through

---

8. Flint Whitlock, *Distant Bugles, Distant Drums, The Union Response to the Confederate Invasion of New Mexico*, (Louisville, CO: University, 2006).

this book to the biographies and lo and behold there was a biography on Ned Wynkoop and it said he was buried at the National Military Cemetery in Santa Fe. Unplanned and unscheduled, but committed to being surprised, of course visiting the cemetery was now added to the list of stops heading north and heading home. This was one of many divine interventions that occurred in such a random way that I had to remind myself, and you, dear reader, that being a pilgrim on a racial justice pilgrimage requires one to be open to be transformed, sometimes by one random moment after another.

One last stop at the Petroglyph National Monument and a late afternoon hike on the Mesa Point Trail at the Boca Negra Canyon to bear witness to petroglyphs made by Ancestral Pueblo people 400-700 years ago. I stayed exploring and discovering a new trail until a park ranger tracked me down and told me I had to leave within minutes as the gate was about to automatically close.

Heading north and ultimately home, I stopped the next day at the National Military Cemetery and discovered Ned's grave in one of the oldest sections of the cemetery that winds itself around long roads built more than a century ago. The random nature of discovering that Ned, Silas' great friend, who died from injuries he sustained from a horse accident at Silas' funeral, reminded me of how deep this friendship must have sustained them both in the most profoundly perilous conditions of their military careers. Part of a band of brothers, who tried to right wrongs, these two, along with Lt. Joe Cramer, and Lt. Col. Samuel Tappan hold a spot in my heart and continue to teach me that the good work of justice is showing up with others, being present and in solidarity with people of color in all the ways I can. I thought of all of that at the grave that day.

A last meal at LaFonda for lunch and an opportunity to take photos of the Palace of the Governors and the historic plaza, which Silas would have seen, as well as LaFonda, which in 1862, was a hotel, and today is the oldest hotel in Santa Fe. After a long day of exploring, I headed up the highway to Las Vegas, NM for the night, for an early morning stop the next day at Fort Union, near Watrous, NM.

Silas wrote a letter here to Walt and he described the Great March of marching 400 miles (or 350 depending on each letter) in 15 days, in February 1862. The conditions must have been horrific, but this is the letter where the soldiers break out into song as they head their way to Fort Union, which today is managed by the National Park Service with active adobe preservation, interpretation, and park ranger talks. On the way to Fort Union, the pilgrim comes across well-worn wagon ruts from previous travelers on the historic Sante Fe Trail in the 19th century heading to Fort Union, or heading to Santa Fe.

The last stop on the pilgrimage was south to Pecos, NM, where the Battle of Glorieta Visitors Center sits right off the highway. This land is where Silas fought in his first battle March 26-28, 1862, with Ned, Samuel Tappen, and the others in the First against the Confederates.

I headed home in silence on the first night of autumn.

Fort Garland and Conejos: Two Days and an Overnight

Pilgrimages got carved out on the calendar for lots of different reasons. This one was because I wanted to meet Eric Carpio, chief community museum officer at History Colorado and museum director at Fort Garland. I headed south again for an early morning visit with Eric, leaving home in the dark for the three-hour trip with a thermos of coffee, and a packed lunch for later. Traveling on I-25 south and again passing Pike's Peak which Silas would have seen on his trip south from Denver, as well as the Spanish Peaks, that he would have also seen, I turned left at Walsenburg, and traveled over LaVeta Pass delighted to have no snow at the summit but could see peaks covered with snow to the south of me. Fort Garland is tucked at the intersection of two historic roadways, one heading south to San Luis, and Taos, NM. The other, going straight, past Mount Blanca, to Alamosa, and then climbs over the Rocky Mountains into the Four Corners of Colorado, New Mexico, Arizona, and Utah.

Eric is creating a whole new way of interpreting this historic fort, with new stories and new interpreters telling the stories. We talked about what does it take to raise children to know right from wrong in these challenging times. "The impact of history and consequence is much more interesting in acknowledging the healing. This museum is not about the answers, it is about asking the questions. How to raise kids with a moral compass? They need to see examples."

On the day I was there, there was a new exhibit on Buffalo Soldiers who were stationed at Fort Garland, as well as a riveting exhibit on Dine (Navajo) enslavement in Conejos, where Silas traveled to, in southern Colorado in the 19th century.

From his overnights at Fort Garland, Silas would have angled off to the left, meandering toward Conejos that would have taken a very long day of travel on horseback. I traveled south, back on the road to Taos, to Colorado's oldest town, San Luis, founded in 1851, and took a right, crossing over the Rio Grande River and the Conejos River then turning left at Manassa. Conejos is located just north of Antonito, which sits on the state line between New Mexico and Colorado. Silas would have stayed near the Ute Indian Agent Lafayette Head's home where he wrote letters from Conejos to his mom and Chivington. He would have seen the oldest church in Colorado in Conejos when he was there in winter-spring 1864.

Today, Our Lady of Guadalupe is a much different church than what he saw, after rebuilding from a fire and more than a century of expanding over time.

Up the road to spend the night in Alamosa, and then a final stop the next day back at Fort Garland before heading home, I raced ahead of a Colorado fall snowstorm to get home before it got dark.

Gilpin County: Two Days of Road Trips

Before the pilgrimage to Silas' beloved Gilpin County, I knew of only two ways to get to Central City, either on the newly built parkway from I-70, or meandering up Clear Creek Canyon on Highway 6. On this pilgrimage, I discovered a third way... the historical route from Golden through Golden Gate Canyon to historic Black Hawk, along the trail that Silas would have traveled!

There were several mysteries I hoped to solve on this day-long pilgrimage, where is Missourie City and where is Mountain City, two locations where Silas wrote a letter. It was a frosty morning when I turned off I-70 headed to Central City to meet up with David Forsyth, executive director of the Gilpin County Historical Society in his office in one of oldest buildings in Central City. It's a little mining town that has changed significantly since Coloradoans voted in gambling in Black Hawk, Central City, and Cripple Creek, but it has tried to retain its 19th century charm.

Forsyth's office is tucked away from the museum, through a curtain, and his ancient office is stacked with files, boxes piled high, and bookcases filled with Colorado history. After a brief visit, he gave me directions to find both of the mysterious missing mining towns, each going in opposite directions in Gilpin County. Heading south to the new parkway, back to where I had originally come from a few hours earlier, and a mile later, I scanned to the right for any signs of a large fenced-in grave that is what is left of Missouie City. I drove back and forth for twenty minutes trying to find the grave and its fence, until I finally called Forsyth, who then joined me in the search. And just as we were going to try another way, there it was, off the highway and a little hike later, we stood at the grave of Clare Delaney, a child, and the site of the bustling 19th century tent city of Missourie City, which would have been tucked under the hillside in front of us. There were many businesses here in Silas' day, and from his letters, he seemed to know everyone and every business well.

From Missourie City, I traveled back to Central City, then drove to Black Hawk, and just as Forsyth suggested, I looked at where these two gambling towns met, and on my left heading down the canyon, there were the stone foundations of once buildings that is the only sign where the thriving town of Mountain City had been. If ever there was a spot Silas called his home away from home, it appears from his letters that it was Gilpin County. The road down Clear Creek Canyon is a twisty, turny canyon road where frost was still on the roadway late in the day, where no sun hits in November.

It was Forsyth who pointed me to the trail Silas would have taken to get to his beloved Gilpin County through Golden, and up Golden Gate Canyon Road crossing the Front Range, and then coming into Blackhawk. So off we went to Golden for a pilgrimage on a trail that Silas traveled. Not nearly as twisty and turny, Golden Gate Canyon Road travels between a wide canyon with picturesque views of the Front Range. Left at the T-intersection, Silas would have seen the spectacular views of the Front Range, and even spot the Rocky Mountain range in the distance, as I did. On this day, snow topped the peaks that made the mountains stand out even more against another robin egg blue Colorado sky. Another meandering stretch, and the pilgrim comes into Blackhawk from the east, and a couple of minutes later, into Central City.

Returning to these places that he loved, and the landscape that he saw, was a reminder of a time when there was joy, surrounded by his Coal Creek friends and brother. It was a place of hard work, and I imagine hard play. So it was with joy that I was there too, surrounded by a place that he loved, and that loved him back.

The Big Sandy, Amache and Bent's Old Fort: Three Days and Two Nights

My first pilgrimage to the Big Sandy, was on opening day on April 28, 2007. Filled with speakers, tribal representatives, state and local dignitaries, the day also included for me, an introduction by State Historian David Haalas to Silas descendant Byron Strom. I have notes on my original program of the day with Byron's phone number.

The superintendent who helped resolve the many differences to get the national historic site to opening day was Dr. Alexa Roberts. Now retired, Dr. Roberts serves on the non-profit Sand Creek Massacre Foundation Board of Directors. She has a perspective like no one else. As a founding member of the foundation, she and the board are committed to the development of the Center for Sand Creek Massacre Studies, public educational initiatives, and what we can learn from violence and genocide in our contemporary world. Another goal the foundation is focused on is understanding generational trauma and what does healing look like. The foundation is currently involved in engaging youth descendants of the Sand Creek Massacre and the Japanese-American incarcerees of the Grenada Relocation Center (Amache National Historic Site), especially in the cross-cultural understanding they are experiencing as Youth Ambassadors to current and future generations. "Listening to these young people is inspiring." Roberts said.

As Rev. Spencer reminds us, claiming a pilgrimage is an invitation to be transformed, and that when we come back home, we are changed by experience, ritual, space, and intention.

All that and more, was part of the pilgrimage that started early from Denver, with a packed lunch, and heading to Pueblo, where Silas was on recruiting service, and then veered left to Sand Creek, with a couple of stops along the way.

Colorado's "incarceration site" (internment camp) for Americans of Japanese descent is now the Amache National Historic Site where 10,000 people were imprisoned between 1942 and 1945.[9] Earlier in the summer I went to Camp Amache, the Grenada War Relocation Center, near Grenada, for a first-time pilgrimage and missed the Amache Museum in Grenada. This time I made a point to schedule this pilgrimage around open hours, and it didn't disappoint. The museum is a sweet collection of artifacts collected by survivors and Descendants of the Amache Internment Camp over the course of decades that tell a story of the struggles of imprisonment. On the day I was there, it included showing home movies of children ice skating at the internment camp. There are items of resistance on display (artifacts for making one's own sake, which was banned), as well as art made in the internment camp.

Following the roadways through what's left of the buildings, and then seeing restored structures is challenging when one thinks of why this camp was even created. The cemetery has graves of those who were imprisoned and died at the camp, and sitting on those cemetery benches was a stark reminder of how humans could be so inhumane to imprison citizens as retaliation.

The landscape, like at Sand Creek, is a wide vista, but unlike

---

9. Amache, "Tell All Stories: The Power of Community," accessed December 20, 2024, https://www.nps.gov/amch/index.htmnps.gov.

at Sand Creek, many of the neighbor's land adjacent to the camp are privately owned. The landscape and its architectural structures help the visitor take in the incredible hardships of being imprisoned. These stories helped illustrate to me what captivity and survival look like, together.

Nightfall came after settling in for the night in Eads, CO, and another early start the next day. The dirt road was a healthy challenge, but I traveled to the locations at the now extinct Bent's Second Fort and the remnants of Fort Lyon. Stones and signage are the only markers of the bustling, diverse communities of Fort Lyon and Bent's Fort. Then to Bent's Old Fort, near LaJunta, where William Bent built a trading empire on the Santa Fe Trail and where he and Southern Cheyenne Owl Woman began their family. Three of their children, Charley, Robert, and George Bent, all were at the Sand Creek Massacre, and survived.

My stop at Bent's Fort included time with National Park Service Superintendent Eric Leonard of the High Plains Group, whose new position includes managing the Sand Creek Massacre National Historic Site, Bent's Old Fort National Historic Site, Amache National Historic Site and Capulin Volcano National Monument. His office in La Junta, CO, next to Bent's Old Fort, is filled with personal photos of he and his family visiting National Parks when he was a child.

Eric brings a profound sacred awareness of the storytelling of violence to his work from serving at Andersonville, a Confederate prisoner of war site and at the American Cold War Park, both National Park Service sites. "I never lose sight of it." Today, the High Plains Group is listed among the International Coalition of Sites of Conscience.[10] He knows that a

---

10. "A Site of Conscience is a place of memory – such as a historic site, place-based museum or memorial – that prevents this erasure from happening in order to ensure a more just and humane future. Nor only do Sites of Conscience provide safe spaces to remember and preserve even the most traumatic memories, but they enable their visitors to make connections be-

healthy percentage of today's visitors to the Sand Creek Massacre Site are "seeking it out to understand it." The National Park Service is the physical caretaker of the Massacre site, and the Cheyenne and Arapaho people are the stewards. "This is a place of healing." Art as resistance.

The next day, the drive from the highway at Chivington, CO (yes, a town has been named after him) is an eight-mile, wide dirt roadway that travels north, much like the way the soldiers would have traveled from Fort Lyon in the darkness to arrive at the Big Sandy at dawn on November 29. Your mind can wander looking at this stretched out landscape that looks like 1864, if you can overlook fencing and farms. There is little that has changed.

Generations of storytelling helped the Massacre site open its gate and welcome Descendants, neighbors and visitors in 2007. I was there among the first visitors on opening day. Today, few visitors find their way here, maybe 6,000 a year. Silas' letter is on an outdoor sign, along with Joseph Cramer's letter next to it, at the Monument Hill Trailhead that takes visitors to the overlook. It's a few minutes of a walk that invites quiet and contemplation. I felt a sense of reverence as I walked along the trail, taking in the cottonwoods that mark the Big Sandy.

The Bluff Trail begins at the overlook and winds its way on the ridge that overlooks the Cheyenne and Arapaho village, where 750 people were camped.[11] Signage along the 1.5-mile trail shares exactly what happened on November 29, 1864. It's a place to be a witness to what happened here.

I had packed a lunch and afterwards sat on the bench over-

---

tween the past and related contemporary human rights issues." https://www.sitesofconscience.org

11. Signage along the Bluff Trail, Sand Creek Massacre National Historic Site, National Park Service.

looking the Repatriation Site to eat my sandwich and take in this sacred place designed by Descendants for the return of the human remains of their ancestors taken from the Massacre site by the soldiers.

It's a solemn sight with no markers, just a boundary. I walked the perimeter as my last intentional moments of this pilgrimage came to an end, and I came home changed. Months before I went on this sacred pilgrimage, I had coffee with Betty Nguyen, Superintendent of Nurturing Leadership and Belonging at the Mountain Sky Conference, United Methodist Church, Denver, CO for some centering time together over coffee. We talked about the work of accountability for the Mountain Sky Conference, the same body of faith, that holds ordained clergy and elders in their standing, that also held John Chivington's call to ministry.

A clergywoman who has served the local church and now serves in the Conference in various roles from logistics around supporting the Spiritual Healing Run to funding partnerships, Betty is committed to reparations and repair work, Descendants work around transformation and solidarity and to discover new ways to not repeat the past. Part of the Conference's work is that "our faith is not extended in systems of power." I asked how do we raise children of faith to know right from wrong? "Have the courage to do what's right with words and action, even when it's hard. I hope in my witness as an Asian American Christian, I still see myself in this story, that ties me to this history."

Lawrence, Osawatomie and Salina: Three Nights, Four Days

Somewhere between the end of my doctoral research in August 2022, and before I wrote my dissertation, I felt a mysterious call to go to Lawrence. I trusted the call. It surprised me, yes, but I've learned to trust call when it speaks. I left early on a September morning, traveled on I-70 to Kansas, pass Fort Riley, where Ned was reassigned after he left Fort Lyon days before the Massacre, and into historic Topeka.

I didn't follow the route Silas took from his home in Coal Creek to Gilpin County on the Smoky Hill Road in 1860, but I saw much of Kansas like he may have seen it without all the new farm equipment and the staggering abundance of corn. After a good rest from a long day of traveling, my first thoughts on the second day of my pilgrimage was that Lawrence is a sweet place to visit. I visited the Plymouth Congregational Church (United Church of Christ) that his parents helped found which looks a lot different today from its hay bale sanctuary origins. I stopped at the Equal Justice Initiative Douglas County Community Remembrance Project sign marking the site of a lynching of three Black men in 1882 by 100 white men. Their names are Issac King, George Robertson and Peter Vinegar. I then meandered up the oldest section of the historic Oak Hill Cemetery where Silas' parents and sisters are buried. And spontaneously discovered the now repatriated Sacred Red Rock that was stolen from the Kaw Nation, placed in Lawrence, and then turned into a monument in 1929 memorializing and naming the dozens of white families on a bronze plaque who arrived beginning in 1854 to keep Kansas free from enslavement. The Sacred Red Rock was finally returned to the Kaw Nation in August 2023 and placed in "Allegawaho Memorial Heritage Park in Council Grove, KS – land purchased by the Kaw Nation that represents the core settlement area of the Kanza's reservation lands in Kansas, prior to their 1873 removal."[12] Being surprised is the unplanned journey of pilgrimage, and nothing surprised me more than hearing the story of the theft of the Sacred Red Rock for purposes of placing a plaque, and celebrating an anniversary of whiteness.

---

12. Anthony Balas, The Kaw Nation Reclaims a Sacred Stone, May 9, 2024, Mellon Foundation, accessed December 20, 2024, https://www.mellon.org/grant-story/the-kaw-nation-reclaim-a-sacred-stonemellon.org.

I drove by the Brown v. Board of Education building managed by the National Park Service, and then stopped at the John and Mary Ritchie home, both in Topeka. Both properties are tied together, with other important historical locations in Kansas on The Kansas African American History Trail. It is a wonderful way to connect with place, landscape, justice, and history and Kansas really needs to be applauded in creating this rare, statewide racial justice journey.

Day three was all about connecting with Silas and John Brown, and traveling to Osawatomie, Brown's home when he was in Kansas where I was delightfully unprepared for the adoration of John Brown at the John Brown Memorial Park. John in bronze statue. John in portrait. John in "Tragic Prelude," on an interpretive sign, painted by John Steuart Curry and is located in the rotunda of the Kansas State Capitol. John in quotes, including his last message before he was executed, "I John Brown am now quite certain that the crimes of this guilty land; will never be purged away but with Blood." For me, this pilgrimage to Osawatomie required time to take this Kansas adoration into heart, as I had never experienced it before. Mention John Brown in a crowd, and one never knows who loves him, or who hates him, who grew up in the South, and who didn't. Here, in the tiny town of Osawatomie made famous by the man committed to violence to dismantle the system of enslavement, I found my people.

I had heard of the new Equal Justice Initiative sign recently installed in Salina, KS, so on my way home, I pulled over at the Salina exit, and ten minutes later stood outside of the library, stopped and breathed in a moment of silence where Dana Adams, a 19-year-old Black man was lynched by 50 white railroad workers on April 20, 1893 at the spot where I stood.

I drove home in darkness that September 2022, on the highway that connects the lynching of Preston Porter Jr., the

Colorado soldiers coming home to Denver after the horrific Massacre, and me.[13]

For me, the power of place has been profound in these pilgrimages and subsequently has influenced the writing of this book in many mysterious ways. Imagine how discovering historical racial justice pilgrimages could open up your world to find voice, and a call to action to stand up, show up, and speak up for justice in our 21st century lives? I've been greatly influenced by writing this book from several authors whose writing about the confluences of justice, place, history, and the memorialization of the past by place in present day, has led me down new trails and paths of understanding. I've then layered upon these new trails and paths with a moral compass pointed towards a young man who challenged systems of oppression, questioned hierarchy, disobeyed orders, and then put himself in harms way traveling across the Masssacre grounds, to then two weeks later to writing a letter of what horrors he witnessed in the acts of violence done by fellow Colorado soldiers.

I am profoundly grateful for the writing of Clint Smith in *How The Word is Passed: A Reckoning With the History of Slavery Across America* and Ta-Nehisi Coates in *The Message*, both of whom have opened my eyes, especially on how to write about violence. I walked away from Smith's work with such reverence on how stories can be told wrong, or that as children we're not told of our own history in the classroom, even though it can be just down the road from our hometowns. As you already know, Smith's words about Confederate monuments in his chapter on Blandford Cemetery, helped me truly put my discovery of the New Mexico Confederate monument, located right off the interstate on land owned by Ted

---

13. The Lynching of Preston Porter Jr., Equal Justice Initiative signage. Preston Porter Jr. was a 15-year-old Black boy who was beaten in the Denver Jail on November 11, then put on a train to Limon, where he was lynched near Lake Station by a white mob that had waited hours for white spectators to gather. https://eji.org/.

Turner, in greater perspective and a more illuminated light. That chapter still haunts me.

Coates, writing of his worldwide pilgrimages with an emphasis on memory, remembrance, and ancestral storytelling, left me wordless after originally listening to this book. I had to own my own copy that I have since marked up in the margins. I especially love when he writes of his parents and growing up in Baltimore, and all the confluences that come on these magnificent pilgrimages with his family, his ancestors, and his past.[14]

Both, Black men. Both, who have written to their children in prior books and later books. Both, who have influenced me in so many known and unknown ways. I have been changed by them.

My theological place in the world has been radically influenced by the work of James H. Cone, and I am grateful to say his name as a Black man who has influenced my own anti-racism theology from his 2004 essay, "Theology's Great Sin: Silence in the Face of White Supremacy."[15] Cones's four elements of what has contributed and continues to create this silence, shook my scholar-activist mind when I discovered his essay during my doctoral work, casually Googling "white silence in churches" while in the library at Phillips Theological Seminary. My work shifted dramatically that day to begin to understand how to dismantle white silence in church, and thanks to Black theologian Regina Shands Stoltzfus, understand how it was historically mantled.[16]

---

14. Ta-Nehisi Coates, *The Message* (New York, NY: One World, 2024).
15. James H. Cone, Theology's Great Sin: Silence in the Face of White Supremacy," Black Theology 2.2: 139-152.
16. Regina Shands Stoltzfus and Tobin Miller Shearer, *Been in the Struggle, Pursuing and Antiracist Spirituality* (Harrisburg, VA: Herald, 2021). Stoltzfus is the director and professor of the Peace, Justice, and Conflict Studies at Goshen College, Goshen, IN.

Epilogue
Meaning Making in the 21st Century

Storytelling changes with time. Different lens get put on and taken off over the course of our past and put on anew. Through the combination of racial justice, or really racial injustice history and generational 21st century interpretive wisdom, we have told the story of a brash and bold young man, who knew right from wrong from a young age and learned to trust it up until he took his last breath.

We've seen the influence of his parents who taught their children about justice as action. They read *Uncle Tom's Cabin* out loud to their children and then moved to Kansas to keep Kansas free from enslavement, inspired by reading Harriet Beecher Stowe's book.

We've seen the influence of being with abolitionists in Kansas at a young age, including traveling with John Brown, and those who worked secretly to break out an Underground Railroad conductor imprisoned in a St. Louis, MO jail. And then some of them attempted to break out two of John Brown's raiders out of the same jail cell where Brown slept waiting for his execution. I've described them as a band of brothers of all ages but committed together to dismantle the system of enslavement at any cost.

We've seen the importance of friends in his life, his willingness to enlist in the American Civil War, his courage to challenge systems within the 19th century military hierarchy. We've wrestled with Silas as an "Indian fighter" and then tried to understand what peacemaking could look like on the Plains in 1864. We have seen the moral courage of knowing the promises of peace that were made to the peaceful camp of Cheyenne and Arapaho people at the Big Sandy and then witness him challenge the system that he had trusted for three years, to disobey orders at the Massacre. We've observed his justice seeking, or "repair work," by writing a letter to his friend Ned with the details of a witness who watched horrific violence and mutilation on elders, women, and children. We've read about his attempt to right the wrongs at the Massacre in the last three letters he wrote and in his testimony at the Congressional Inquiry. We've read time and time again, in lots of different ways, about his longings to get home.

We read the last moments of his life as justice in action as he runs into the dark Denver night April 23, 1865 after hearing shots fired in the distance.

I hope there are places where you've been inspired by Silas, discovered yourself in his story, seen his humanity and imperfection, as well as found your racial justice voice, possibly for the first time. Maybe you've pledged to write letters seeking justice for others. Maybe you want to make a pilgrimage to the Big Sandy. Maybe you will commit to going to museums tell your story and be part of storytelling in new ways with family, friends, and colleagues in community because everyone's story matters and it needs to be told. Maybe you will want to stop by and visit Silas at his grave the next time you're in Denver. As this book comes to the end, you kind reader have an opportunity to bear witness to Silas' life in ways that are now part of your story.

We've journeyed not just as witnesses to his life, but as witnesses to some of the most difficult, painful and horrific moments in Colorado history that "we" are heirs to, 160 years later.[1]

As a white clergywoman of European descent, and a descendent of great-grandparents who arrived in America through Ellis Island as immigrants, I have discovered over the course of time that being accountable to the past as a white person, and to a denominational racial unjust past, has been part of how I grew into activist and scholarly work of dismantling white silence. I lament and grieve the places in my own denominational historical past as part of that accountability and I work in dismantling the silence that still keeps these racially unjust stories from being told in sanctuaries from coast to coast on Turtle Island. After accountability, and lament or grief work, I seek for where hope and healing may be found or nurtured.[2] I ask myself what do I need to heal from, whatever healing may look like that day, or the next day, or the next week or month. Because healing is not stagnant, it is ongoing work that requires intentionality and mindfulness. Over time, I have found that some of the places of profound healing, truth telling, accountability and finding hope have been found in community with others, much like what I read in Silas' letters.

Today, there is a new truth telling place, or actually a restarting truth telling place, where the United Methodist Church, the ancestral denomination of Chivington and Evans, and the Sand Creek Massacre Descendants are carving out a way forward into the future with reconciliation and hope. The

---

1. "We are heirs to" is language first heard by, and attributed to former Bishop Elaine Stanovsky, Mountain Sky Conference, United Methodist Church.
2. Accountability, lament-grief, and healing work, is the cornerstone of my Doctor of Ministry work at Phillips Theological Seminary, "Dismantling White Silence in United Church of Christ Churches Using Storytelling of White Nineteenth Century Ancestors of Faith and Resistance who Stood Up, Showed Up and Spoke Up With People of Color," February 2023.

new United Methodist Responses to the Sand Creek Massacre Team met for the first time in 2024 and is committed to the ongoing work of reconciliation in the United Methodist Church, with Cheyenne and Arapaho Descendants. An updated version of a 2016 resolution in the United Methodist Church was adopted by the 2024 General Conference that laid out specific actions the church could undertake to work toward a true reconciliation. On that list is "encouraging the return of Native American artifacts and remains related to the massacre [Massacre]."

We have read in Silas' letters about the horrific mutilation of Cheyenne and Arapaho bodies after they were killed. We have read from George Bent's letters about the painful recognition of human remains of friends. We heard from the High Plains Group superintendent of human remains that have been repatriated to the land. In his doctoral dissertation, historian Gary L. Roberts identifies Colorado soldiers by name who mutilated those who were killed. These stories have had a profound effect on me, this book, and the repair work that is yet to be done.

As we come to the end of our story, I invite anyone who has been the recipient, passed down through generations, of human remains or objects taken from the Sand Creek Massacre site, to repatriate them and return them to the place where they were taken.

The public law that authorized the Massacre site in 2000 contains a provision, requiring that the National Park Service dedicate a portion of the federally acquired land within the site to the establishment and operation of a site for certain items (e.g., Native American human remains, associated funerary objects, sacred objects, objects of cultural patrimony) that are repatriated under the Native American Graves Protection and Repatriation Act or any other provision of law may be interred, reinterred, preserved, or otherwise protected. For those actions the National Park Service works with the Tribes in accordance with the law.[3]

As I read the stories of these sacred items being taken from the Massacre site, I came to slowly realize that there is no way to know how many human remains there are in the homes of people who may have never known how to or had an invitation to return them. My invitation to you is to return these sacred human remains and sacred objects that were taken by Colorado soldiers, your ancestors. There is no shame in this, nor is there judgement, but it *is* doing the right thing. Maybe its repair work to right an ancestor's wrong. Descendants of soldiers inherited something that really is not yours and now is the time to let it go back to the land and the people.

Descendants of soldiers can begin their own repatriation process by contacting the Tribal Consultation Office at Bent's Fort at hpg_tribal_consultations@nps.gov. They will forward the next steps of the repatriation process to return these sacred items back to the place where they need to be.

Finally, there is grief and loss in the storytelling of history, though it rarely gets mentioned, or interpreted, there has been great loss and grief in this story; you know the places where your heart was touched and grieved a loss. How we find ourselves in this story of grief, discovering a call of action for justice, and where we can tell our own stories, maybe in writing letters, is where we can find hope together. We can also find hope in singing in community the songs of justice and peace, hope and transformation.The civil rights movement taught us songs of hope, and here's one Vincent Harding taught me...

> We are building up a new world, we are building up a new world, we are building up a new world, builders must be strong. Courage sisters, don't get weary, cour-

---
3. Email from Eric Leonard to author, December 20, 2024.

age brothers, don't get worried, courage people, don't get worried, though the way we long.⁴

Go forth and build up a new world with abundant blessings in the racial justice work you are called to do, and be in community with others to nourish each other in this holy work.

May we all try to be a bit more like Silas.

---

4. Vincent Harding at Wild Goose, 2013, accessed December 30, 2024. Sung to the tune of "We Are Climbing Jacob's Ladder. https://www.youtube.com/watch?v=TC7pv-a0uUY. Harding was professor of religion and social transformation at Iliff School of Theology, Denver, CO, from 1981-2004. In retirement, Harding returned to Iliff as a guest professor when I was a student from 2006-2009.

Afterword

Nancy Niero's treatise on the life of Silas Stillman Soule is not, strictly speaking, a biography. It is a search for meaning. Its core is the collection of known letters written by Soule. That within itself is a significant contribution. As anyone who has attempted to write a biography knows, the verifiable facts about a life alone are important, but the existence of a body of personal papers — letters, diaries, journals, even reminiscences — have the effect of revealing the core values of one's subject in a more personal way.

Depth, principles, prejudices, self-awareness, passion (or lack thereof), and all things that matter in defining the character of a life, reveal themselves far more than factual information can alone. Silas Soule was the sort of man who revealed his very soul — no pun intended — in warm, personal, honest prose, even when jocular, self-effacing or plainly angry. Silas gave us the gift of letters that can be used to test the broader historical record by taking a more intimate measure of a man.

Niero's commentary on the letters and the man who wrote them is intensely personal as well. She dares to reveal herself in what she has learned during her quest to find and understand the man over thirty years of research, and, ultimately who she found him to be. She never claims that Soule was a man without flaws. He admitted as much himself, and in doing so made himself more credible as a good man. More than defining Soule as a person, Niero dares to show the questions life raises for all people who would live principled lives.

Niero first met Silas Soule in a stairwell to the basement of the Colorado State Historical Society (now History Colorado) in Denver. She was a new employee, and she asked her guide about the man who was keeping watch in the stairwell. Her guide introduced him as Captain Silas Stillman Soule and mentioned his role in exposing the Sand Creek Massacre. Nancy knew about Sand Creek, and she was intrigued by Soule's effort to expose it as an atrocity. It was his courage to speak out that intrigued her and sparked a quest that influenced her personally as well as professionally.

As she points out, she later served as the first director of the Fairmount Heritage Foundation. She found Soule's grave in the G. A. R. section of the Fairmount Cemetery. She was still interested in Soule and wondered how the larger community could find meaning in his life and "accountability" for people of good will and faith, especially in light of the knowledge that the author of the Sand Creek Massacre, John Milton Chivington, was a Methodist minister. She could not let go of Soule's story. Over the years she studied his life, met descendants of "Sile" like Byron Strom, walked where Soule had walked, stood where he had stood, came to know the descendants of the Cheyenne and Arapaho who died at Sand Creek, and deepened her determination to show others who Silas Soule was and why his example is relevant for every generation.

Silas Stillman Soule inherited his passionate and adventurous spirit naturally enough. His ancestral forebear in America, George Soule, made passage as a teacher and servant on the *Mayflower* with other Pilgrims in 1620 and his signature is there with the others on the Mayflower Compact. Almost two hundred years passed with Soules in New England, before Silas's father, Amasa Soule, was born in Woolwich, Maine, on February 10, 1804. Amasa was not an educated man, but he grew up a searcher for truth, with strong views about right and wrong. He was by faith and instinct a man committed to justice and the service of others.

Amasa was an early convert to the cause of abolishing slavery (which was not popular at the time even among most anti-slavery New Englanders). But he named his first son William Lloyd Garrison Soule, making clear just where he stood. His second son, Silas, was born on July 26, 1838, into a Boston household of faith, service, and justice. Amasa was a good teacher of all three. He rejected any compromise with what he perceived as evil. His four surviving children, including his daughters, Emily and Annie, were weaned on Garrison's abolitionist newspaper, *The Liberator*, and Harriet Beecher Stowe's *Uncle Tom's Cabin*, underscored by their father's admonitions about courage and the need for action in support of principle.

Silas absorbed it all, but he was different. He never struck people as particularly pious or self-righteous as boy or man. He even described himself as "wild." Silas was confident, open-minded, funny, likeable. He was passionate in his beliefs and committed to the principles his father taught him. That meant that it was not enough to be opposed to slavery. Ending slavery was the goal, and that meant action. Amasa proved that when he moved to Kansas to join the fight against slavery in the wake of the Kansas-Nebraska Act. Young Silas's personality did not change, but he was ready to fight the good fight.

He joined Samuel Walker's free-state militia and was involved in the Underground Railroad assisting runaway slaves. Later, he participated in the rescue of Dr. John Doy, an abolitionist leader, met John Brown and was recruited for a failed plan to rescue Brown after his raid at Harper's Ferry. After Brown's execution, four men from the Doy rescue party were recruited by James Montgomery to save two of Brown's followers who were waiting to be hanged. Silas was the key person who spoke with the two prisoners. Even though the effort failed, Thomas Wentworth Higginson, a key leader of the plan to rescue Brown and his associates, praised Silas as "a man of great resources." He was near the center of the radical abolitionist movement. On a trip back east, he met other leaders of the movement and a writer, whose work he admired, named Walt Whitman. He visited his sister Emily in New England and decided to return to Kansas.

When Silas reached Lawrence, he learned that his brother, Will, had departed for the gold fields of Colorado with a group of locals. He found that Will had purchased a quartz mill and was optimistic about mining prospects. Silas took less than a week to decide to join his brother to chase El Dorado. With a naivete bordering on innocence, Silas's destiny had changed.[1] His character had not. He slipped easily into the frontier communities of Denver and Central City, worked hard, participated in community life, and followed his interests in literature and theatre, indulged in more traditional frontier pleasures. His affable ways, his wit, and his honest approach to life assured his popularity. When the Civil War finally came in April 1861, he quickly decided to strike another blow at slavery, enlisting in the first Colorado Infantry (later the First Colorado Cavalry), as First Lieutenant in Company K, and he soon saw action in the New Mexico campaign against the Confederate advance to claim Colorado gold for the Southern cause.

---

1. This brief review of Silas Soule's early years is drawn largely from Tom Bensing, *Silas Soule: A Short Eventful Life of Moral Courage* (Indianapolis: Dog Ear Publishing, 2012), 1-42. Bensing's book is the best available biography of Soule, thorough and thoughtful, and fills in some important details.

Soule proved his mettle in the New Mexico Campaign of 1862, despite a command that was seriously divided in its loyalties between the regimental commander John P. Slough, and Major John M. Chivington, the regimental major. The cold and quarrelsome Slough had his shortcomings as an officer and clashed with the bold and charismatic Chivington from the beginning. Slough unexpectedly resigned as regimental commander in protest of orders to retire to Fort Union after Glorieta and with rumors rampant that he had been fired upon by his own troops during the fighting. He would nonetheless be promoted to Brigadier General and served most of the rest of the war in Virginia.

General Edward Canby, bypassed Lt. Col. Samuel F. Tappan in favor of Major Chivington, based on a petition signed by officers of the First Colorado. Silas Soule was not one of them. Silas had known and respected Tappan during the Kansas troubles, and he remained loyal to his associate because of their past relationship. Still, he was drawn to Chivington, a six-foot, four-inch bear of a man with an ego to match. Chivington was a Methodist minister who refused to accept the regimental chaplaincy in favor of a soldier's role. He was flamboyant and ambitious. Now touted as the hero of Glorieta and nicknamed "The Fighting Parson," his military and political ambitions overpowered his calling to the pulpit.

Silas got to know him better when he was appointed Chivington's Acting Assistant Adjutant General. Soule's charm and manner were infectious, and he was appointed a recruiter in Denver. The division within the regiment remained a problem, mostly because of Chivington's penchant for quarrels with other officers, including Tappan, but Soule somehow trusted Chivington. While Chivington seethed over the lack of action and promotion, Silas enjoyed the social life of Denver, until he learned of William Clarke Quantrill's attack on Lawrence, Kansas, where Soule's family remained including Will, who had returned to Lawrence and taken the job of town marshal.

Silas could not go to his family's aid, but he renewed his efforts as a recruiter so effectively that Chivington sent him to Fort Garland in southern Colorado to enlist Mexicans in the area and use his charm to persuade veterans to reenlist. Ironically, the assignment landed him in the middle of Chivington's feud with Tappan, then the commander at Fort Garland. Somehow, Soule managed to avoid offending either, while he worked to ease the tensions at Garland and complete his recruiting mission.

Thoroughly miserable because of the multiple controversies at Fort Garland, he urged Chivington to recall him to Denver. Chivington did and promoted Soule to the rank of Captain besides. Remarkably, he returned to Denver with Sam Tappan, who had been granted a leave to attend to business back east following the death of his father. Tappan and Soule visited mining claims they shared near Central City and Blackhawk while Soule recruited in the camps. He had that rare ability to maintain his relationship with Tappan, while respecting Chivington to the point that he was considered one of Chivington's "favorites" along with Major Edward W. Wynkoop, another former Kansan, and a few others. Chivington even recommended that Soule be considered for the rank of Lt. Col in a new regiment being organized in Idaho

By the spring of 1864, Colorado was awash with rumors and predictions of imminent Indian troubles. So far, there were far more rumors than clashes, including a couple of ill-advised incidents in April. Still, Governor John Evans and Colonel Chivington fed the growing fear in the mining camps. From his location in and near Denver, Soule heard the reports and saw the mood among the settlers. A major flood on Cherry Creek destroyed his office and most of the City of Denver, as well. In June the murders of the Hungate family near Denver threw the city into a panic, and Governor Evans predicted the worst.

With his promotion, Soule was transferred to Fort Lyon on the Arkansas River as commander of Company D of the First Colorado with Ned Wynkoop as his post commander. Soule and Wynkoop likely knew little about the political shenanigans of Chivington, who now had his eyes set on Colorado statehood and a political career in the U. S. Congress. Soule and Wynkoop supported both and concentrated on their new responsibilities at Fort Lyon patrolling the Arkansas route against a predicted Indian threat.

They were not "Indian fighters" yet, but Wynkoop and Soule likely shared at least some of the prejudices of Colorado settlers. Tensions with the tribes increased in July primarily in Kansas and Nebraska. On August 7, 1864, on the Little Blue River and Plum Creek in Nebraska, bloody assaults were unleashed and extended up the Platte. By then, Major Wynkoop and Captain Soule were drawn into the conflict between Fort Lyon and Fort Larned. They had heard of Governor John Evans's proclamations to the Indians, and newspapers reported the progress of the campaign for statehood. They knew as well that Governor Evans had been granted the right to organize the Third Colorado Cavalry, a 100-day Regiment, to fight the "hostiles." It was also clear that even the officers at Fort Lyon were divided in their loyalties. Chivington was being criticized by others as well, including General Samuel Ryan Curtis, the commander of the Department of Kanas, for spending more time campaigning for statehood than fighting Indians. Curtis removed Fort Lyon from the District of Colorado and created the new District of the Upper Arkansas because of Chivington's dilatory tactics.

Still, when Black Kettle, the Cheyenne chief, sent a message offering to make peace and to surrender captives in response to the governor's proclamation. Wynkoop made the fateful decision to meet with the Cheyennes and Arapahos to try to end the conflict and recover the captives. It was a bold move, but the expedition returned to Lyon with seven Cheyenne and Arapaho chiefs and four young prisoners captured on the Little Blue and Plum Creek. The captives included Laura Roper, age 17, Ambrose Asher, age 7, Isabelle Eubanks, age 3, all taken on the Little Blue, and Dannie Marble, age 9, taken at Plum Creek. The chiefs who accompanied Wynkoop's command back to Lyon included three Cheyenne council chiefs, Black Kettle, White Antelope, and Bull Bear (a leader of the Dog Soldier society that had been admitted to the Council as a band), and four Arapaho chiefs, Neva (the brother of Left Hand, the leading voice for peace among the Southern Arapaho chiefs), No-ta-nee, Bosse, and Heap of Buffalo.

General Curtis was distracted, locked in a major campaign with General Sterling Price's Confederate forces in Kansas and Missouri. Wynkoop was not pleased with the command of the Upper Arkansas District. Wynkoop reasoned that John Evans, as Ex Officio Superintendent of Indian Affairs for Colorado, needed to be involved in the talks. Chivington had also told Wynkoop to inform him of any important developments. Wynkoop had more confidence in Chivington than the new commander of the Upper Arkansas. Accordingly, he sent a message to Chivington that he was bringing the chiefs and captives to Denver to talk peace, which technically violated department orders.

Neither Chivington nor Evans were pleased with the news. Both hoped for a military solution, although they had different ideas of what needed to be done. The Camp Weld conference with the chiefs was perfunctory, but the chiefs and their escorts left convinced that peace was at hand. Wynkoop and Soule still trusted Chivington, and when the first Arapahos and Cheyennes arrived at Fort Lyon to accept the terms of the Weld Conference, Soule wrote a lengthy letter to Chivington advising him that large numbers of Indians had come in, following the instructions given at Camp Weld.

Soule thought he was congratulating Chivington. He did not know that both Chivington and Evans had other designs. Chivington's command had dwindled in numbers after the districts were redrawn. General Curtis had lost confidence in him, there were no active hostilities on the plains, and Chivington's commission was due to expire in a matter of weeks.

Chivington's only hope was a quick victory, and Soule's letter confirmed his only real target. Evans, humiliated by the defeat of statehood, headed to Washington D. C. to seek a major campaign against the plains tribes and to explain his course of action in Colorado. Chivington kept his plan to attack the Indians at Fort Lyon secret, so that when Soule and a patrol from Fort Lyon encountered Chivington's column of the Third Colorado Cavalry and a battalion of the First Colorado stationed near Denver, on the road west of Lyon early on the morning of November 28, he was stunned.

Wynkoop, who had made the best of his situation, had been replaced as commander at Fort Lyon by Major Scott J. Anthony, who was unhappy with the situation there. He instructed the chiefs to move their people away from the fort to Sand Creek to await further instructions. When Chivington met Soule on the road, he still believed that the Cheyennes and Arapahos were at Fort Lyon.

On the morning of November 28, 1864, Soule realized the Third's target. By the time he reached Fort Lyon with the column, he was so infuriated and vocal that his fellow officers feared he would be arrested, but several 0f them condemned Chivington's intent with such fervor, that Chivington screamed, "Damn any man in sympathy with Indians!" Lieutenant George Hawkins resigned his commission and refused to join the expedition.

The combined forces, reinforced by the Lyon Battalion led by Major Anthony, left Fort Lyon the same evening on a night march to the "place of "safety" on Sand Creek some forty miles northeast of Lyon, arriving near daybreak the following morning. Chivington's command struck the village without warning. Before the attack began, Captain Soule told his men who they were attacking. "Well, we won't fire a shot today," Private Charles Lynch said, with others agreeing. They rode into the fight determined to keep their word.[2] Lt. Cramer later wrote Wynkoop that when he saw what was happening, "I got so mad I swore I would not burn powder, and I did not."

When Lt. Horace Baldwin was ordered to fire the howitzer battery from Fort Lyon, the shells exploded high, causing many to believe that he deliberately did so to avoid as much damage as possible. The "Thirdsters," as members of the Third Regiment were called, were afraid they were going to be held back in the fight, lost discipline, and the "battle" quickly became a bloodbath that fell heaviest on non-combatants who were shot indiscriminately, scalped, and mutilated.

Still, Chivington claimed a glorious victory. Back at Fort Lyon, Chivington strutted and claimed that he had proved himself better than General Harney or Kit Carson. Soule railed at Chivington's perfidy with his fellow officers, including Sam Tappan who had just returned from his extended leave back East. Chivington left his command and hurried back to Denver to celebrate his "great victory," but a plan to expose Sand Creek as a massacre was also taking shape.

Soule's role was central to both sides. Chivington singled Soule out in his first report to General Curtis for "conduct" at Sand Creek that proved "him more in sympathy with the

---

2. Pam Milavec, "Jesse Haire: Unwilling Indian Fighter," *Prologue* (Summer 2011): 42-48.

Indians than with the whites." Soule's letter to Ned Wynkoop, along with the letters of Joe Cramer to Wynkoop and others, reached high into the circles of power. Cramer wrote Wynkoop, "Col. Tappan is after them for all that is out."

With Tappan's connections in Washington and Denver, other public officials in Colorado Territory quietly joined the fight, and soon the story found its way to the floor of Congress and into eastern newspapers. On January 10, the Joint Committee on the Conduct of the War, was instructed to investigate Sand Creek. By the time he was transferred to Denver as the Assistant Provost Marshal, Soule had become a target of angry Thirdsters who blamed him for delayed pay and confiscated property pending investigation, as well as for exposing their victory as an atrocity.

When a military commission was convened to investigate Sand Creek, Lieutenant Colonel Tappan, as the highest-ranking officer in the district who was not at Sand Creek, was presiding officer. Soule and Cramer were the first two witnesses. Their testimony was devastating, and threats against them increased. Silas's behavior hardly changed. He was still open, generous, and friendly to Denver's citizens and veterans, clinging to the principles he had been taught those years before at his father's knee. He had seen a great wrong done, and his efforts to make things right by exposing Sand Creek and seeing justice done were unrelenting. He knew the dangers of his course, but he never hesitated.

In late March, Soule shared his fears with Captain George F. Price, the new District Inspector, on a ride to Central City. He told Price that he "fully expected to be killed because of his testimony" and that after he was killed, "his character would be assailed and an attempt made to destroy his testimony" before the commission. This was a different tone than he had used when he wrote his mother not to worry about him.

Soule found solace and support in the love of a woman, Hersa Coberly. Hersa's father, James Coberly, ran a popular boarding house, and stage stop near Huntsville, Colorado where he also served as a sutler for the distribution of supplies to the military. He was killed by Indians near Franktown in August 1864. Hersa's brother, Joe had joined the Third Colorado when the regiment was organized and participated in the Sand Creek affair. Hersa was witty and popular, working at Coberly's for her parents. After her father's death, her mother moved to Huntsville. The romance between Silas and Hersa began at some point in 1864. They were kindred spirits from the start. It was not surprising that they fell in love, despite the disapproval of Hersa's mother. She and Silas were married on April Fool's Day, 1865. Their marriage was but a sweet moment, however. On the night of April 23, 1865, Silas Soule was murdered on the streets of Denver.

Silas was escorting Hersa home after an evening on the town when they heard gunfire. Soule saw his wife safely home on Curtis Street, and as provost marshal, he rushed to the sound of the shots. Armed only with a derringer, Soule encountered two unassigned recruits of the Second Colorado Cavalry. Williamson Morrow and Charles W. Squier. Both had pistols drawn, and he drew his derringer. Charles W. Squier fired first, the bullet crashing into Soule's face and lodging in his brain. Soule managed to fire a shot in the melee which tore into Squier's gun hand. Squier fled after his companion, leaving his bloody revolver where he dropped it.

It did not go without notice that Chivington had offered a $500 reward for killing Indians and their sympathizers. Tappan, Wynkoop, and others in high positions and low were convinced that Squier was an assassin. A large crowd attended Silas's funeral, and the Reverend H. B. Hitchings gave a moving, but carefully worded eulogy extolling Soule's record as a soldier and demanding that if there had been a plot to murder him that the citizens and soldiers "discover and crush it."

Tappan adjourned the military investigation for several days because of Soule's death, but when it reconvened, Chivington proved Soule's prophecy by introducing a deposition from a freighter named Lipman Meyer, which accused Soule of being a coward, a drunkard, a liar, and a thief. Tappan was enraged. He refused to admit the *deposition and reminded the court of Soule's conversation* with Captain Price. Still, Chivington's case depended primarily on discrediting Soule and other witnesses who had testified. On May 30, 1865, the commission completed its work.

Squier had been arrested in New Mexico by James D. Cannon, an officer who had also been present at Sand Creek as part of the Lyon Battalion. Squier was escorted back to Denver to await trial for murder and desertion. Cannon died of an apparent suicide under mysterious circumstances, which led Wynkoop and others to believe that he, like Soule, was murdered. Squier was kept under close guard and heavily shackled, but before he could be tried he escaped a second time, clearly with outside help. Previously, he had been known in Denver, if at all, as a troublesome unassigned recruit of the Second Colorado Cavalry who spent his time carousing and being arrested once before, possibly by Soule. It turned out that he had friends in high places. His brother, Ephraim George Squier, was a successful businessman, author of books on American archeology, a well-placed figure in Centra American politics, an entrepreneur in the construction of the first railroad across Honduras and Nicaragua, editor of *Frank Leslie's Illustrated Newspaper*, and well-connected in American political circles. His other primary task was helping to keep his brother out of trouble.

Charles was intelligent, but erratic, constantly moving from one thing to another, and increasingly unstable. He had served as a Captain in the 74th New York Regiment of the Excelsior Brigade early in the war. By 1863 he had fallen into a pattern of moving from one place to another. Squandering a promising military career, he worked as an engineer for a railroad which carried him to Colorado. There, he was arrested for shooting Mariano Medina, a well-known mountain man and pioneer of Colorado. He was convicted of attempted murder, but the case was thrown out on a technicality.

He had fallen into the habit of threatening generals, politicians, and others, which worried Ephraim, but when Charles got arrested for shooting Silas Soule, his brother intervened on his behalf, enlisting the aid of General David Sickles and even General John Pope. Charles escaped from a jail where he was in chains. Who helped him was never revealed. He wandered over the next few years as erratic and unstable as ever, even joining the army again as "Charles Wesley, in Georgia during Reconstruction. He traveled back to Central America with Ephraim helping him. Eventually, his brother secured Charles a job with the Erie Railroad. On Thanksgiving Day 1869, he suffered serious injuries trying to prevent a train wreck. Squier died on December 9, 1869, of his injuries, and was buried with full military honors for his service as Captain in the Excelsior Brigade during 1861-63.[3]

Eventually, the Tappan commission's report was forwarded to Washington, D. C. but, although the Judge Advocate General described Sand Creek as a "cowardly and coldblooded slaughter", he ruled that Chivington could not be tried because he was no longer in the military service. Two Congressional Committees also condemned Sand Creek, making it one of the most investigated actions of the Civil War. Chivington's life after Sand Creek was a shabby display of questionable behavior. He eventually moved back to Colorado where many

---

3. Bensing, 138-140.

welcomed him as a hero.[4] Until his death, he continued to defend himself by saying, "I stand by Sand Creek."

Silas Soule never saw himself as a hero, but his moral courage and commitment to justice defined who he was. That is why Cheyenne and Arapaho people remember him to this day. The words of Soule and Joe Cramer that prompted the investigations into Sand Creek in 1865 were the same words that pushed the U. S. Senate to pass the bill creating the Sand Creek Massacre National Historic Site in November 2000, the same words that the Cheyenne and Arapaho ponder at the place where Soule died, every year at the annual healing run from the Sand Creek site to the state capital.

The letters of Silas Soule inspired Nancy Niero to spend decades seeking to understand the man who wrote them. She has shown us how Silas Soule changed her life and priorities and reminds all of us why it matters.

-Gary L. Roberts
Emeritus Professor of History,
Abraham Baldwin Agricultural College (Tifton, Georgia)

---

4. For a detailed account of Chivington's post-Sand Creek life, see, Gary L. Roberts, *Massacre at Sand Creek: How Methodists Were Involved in an American Tragedy* (Nashville: Abingdon Press, 2016), 189-204.

Acknowledgements

I discovered Silas' grave at Riverside Cemetery, in Denver in 2002, as the new executive director at Fairmount Heritage Foundation, the historic preservation organization at Denver's two historic cemeteries, Fairmount and Riverside. Thanks to former President Kelly Briggs, Cliff Dougal, and Chuck Counts.

I am incredibly grateful to the cloud of witnesses who saw the storyteller of Silas in me, some even 15 years ago at Iliff School of Theology. Deep gratitude to Dr. Debbie Creamer, Glenn Duggin, Dr. Julie Todd, and Rev. Dr. Richard Ward.

Grateful for the Colorado Historical Society, Denver Public Library Western History Collection, Kansas State Historical Society for my original research 15 years ago.

So many thanks to the scholars at Phillips Theological Seminary, especially Rev. Dr. Lisa Barnett and Katherine Casey.

I had made a commitment early on to interview historical interpreters of the 21st century, hopefully in-person, rather than tell the story of Silas with book authors of the last generation about the landscape of Silas' life. I wanted to literally be with those who were interpreting history for us now, and for me, to ask questions of how we make meaning out of events like the Sand Creek Massacre in the 21st century. The list is long of these saints who never said no, always said yes, sometimes with two or three conversations, and shared countless hours in helping me become the best storyteller I could be. I could not have written this book without Dr. Loring Abeyta, Pastor Dustin Adkins, Sam Bock, Dr. Rita Nakashima Brock, Eric Carpio, Ruben Figaroa, David Forsyth, Trinidad Gallegos, Eric Leonard, Mario Medina, Byron Parker, Dr. Alexa Roberts, Dr. Gary Roberts, Virginia Sanchez, Rev. Bonnie Spencer, John Taylor, and Karl Zimmerman.

Grateful for Kristin and Lewis Wyman at the Library of Congress; Elizabeth, Hannah Rose, Will and Erin at the University of Denver Special Collections; the front desk staff at the Denver Public Library Special Collections and Archives and Craig Haggit.

I am grateful beyond words for those who showed up at Silas' grave all those birthdays ago when I started reading this collection of letters at his grave on his birthday, including Pastor Dustin Adkins, Rev. Wayne Laws, Eric McEuen, Diane Sandman, and Dan Whittemore.

I am profoundly grateful to Chris Driscoll, my publisher at Exact Rush, who took a leap of faith in me, and I in him. May we scholars and academics all be able to have a publisher who brings the wisdom, creativity, enthusiasm and passion that Chris brings to this book. His commitment to financial equity for scholars in the books we write is an inspiration.

Finally, this book would never have been written if it had not been for the generous spirit of Byron Strom. I am profoundly grateful for his journey with me, more than 20 years now. His gift of sharing Silas' letters with not just me, but with scholars, authors, and museums, speaks to his deepest desire to invite the world to know who this amazing man is, a profound desire that I share with him. His generosity, and his family's preservation over four generations of these letters speaks to his love of history as a storyteller, and his quest to keep sharing the painful and horrific day at Sand Creek on November 29, 1864.

Bibliography

Blankenship, Anne M. *Christianity, Social Justice, and the Japanese American Incarceration during World War II.* Chapel Hill, NC: University of North Carolina, 2016.

Brock, Rita Nakashima and Gabriella Lettini. *Soul Repair, Recovering from Moral Injury after War.* Boston, MA: Beacon, 2012.

Budde, Mariann Edgar, Episcopal Bishop of Washington. *How We Learn To Be Brave, Decisive Moments in Life and Faith.* New York, NY: Avery, 2023.

Coates, Ta-Nehisi Coates, *The Message*, New York, NY: One World, 2024.

Dr. Raymond G. Carey Manuscript Collection, University of Denver Special Collections and Archives, Denver, CO.

Du Bois, W.E. Burghardt. *John Brown.* Philadelphia, PA: The Estate of W.E.B. Du Bois, 1972.

Fitzsimons, Matt. *The Counterfeiters of Bosque Redondo, Slavery, Silver and the U.S. War Against the Navajo Nation.* Charleston, SC: History Press, 2022.

Genoways, Ted. *Walt Whitman and the Civil War, America's Poet During the Lost Years of 1860-1862.* Berkeley, CA: University of California, 2009.

Halaas. David Fridtjof Halaas and Andrew E. Masich. *Halfbreed, The Remarkable True Story of George Bent.* Cambridge, MA: De Capo, 2004.

Higginson, Thomas Wentworth. *Cheerful Yesterdays.* The American Negro, His History and Literature. New York, NY: Arno Press, 1968.

Hinton, Richard J. *John Brown and His Men.* The American Negro, His History and Literature, New York, NY: Arno Press, 1968.

Historical Map Collection, Western History and Genealogy, Denver Public Library, Denver, CO.

Hyde, George. *Life of George Bent Written From His Letters.* Norman, OK: University of Oklahoma, 1968.

Kelman, Ari. *A Misplaced Massacre, Struggling Over the Memory of Sand Creek.* Cambridge, MA, First Harvard University, 2013.

Loeb, Paul Rogat. *The Impossible Will Take A Little While.* New York, NY: Basic, 2014.

Menakem, Resmaa. *My Grandmother's Hands, Racialized Trauma and the Pathway to Mending Our Hearts and Bodies.* Las Vegas, NV: Central Recovery, 2017.

National Archives, Fort Garland, Aug. 1855-Dec. 1872, Returns from U.S. Military Posts, 1800-1916.

National Archives, Military Records, Silas Stillman Soule, 1861-1865.

Newcomb, Steven T. *Pagans in the Promised Land.* Chicago, IL: Clergy Review, 2008.

Reynolds, David S. *John Brown Abolitionist, The Man Who Killed Slavery, Sparked the Civil War, and Seeded Civil Rights.* New York, NY, Knopf, 2005.

Roberts, Gary L. *Massacre at Sand Creek, How Methodists Were Involved in an American Tragedy,* Nashville, TN: Abingdon, 2016.

Roberts, Gary Leland. "Sand Creek: Tragedy and Symbol." Doctor of Philosophy diss., University of Oklahoma, Norman, 1984.

Roberts, Gary L. and David Fridtjof Halaas. "The Soule-Cramer Sand Creek Massacre Letters." Colorado Heritage, Winter, 2001.

Sanchez, Virginia. *Pleas and Petitions, Hispano Culture and Legislative Conflict in Territorial Colorado.* Louisville, CO: University Press, 2020.

Silas Soule Manuscript Collection, Stephen Hart Library, Colorado Historical Society, Denver, CO.

Smith, Clint. *How the Word Is Passed, A Reckoning With The History of Slavery Across America.* New York, NY: Hachette Book Group, 2021.

Stoltzfus, Regina Shands and Tobin Miller Shearer, *Been In The Struggle,* Harrisonburg, VA: Herald, 2021.

Taylor, John. *Bloody Valverde, A Civil War Battle on the Rio*

Grande, February 21, 1862. Albuquerque, NM: University of New Mexico, 1995.

Edrington, Thomas S. and John Taylor. *The Battle of Glorieta Pass, A Gettysburg in the West, March 26-28, 1862.* Albuquerque, NM: University of New Mexico, 1998.

The Illustrated Miners' Hand-book and Guide to Pike's Peak with a New and Reliable Map, Showing all the Routes, and the Gold Regions of Western Kansas and Nebraska. Saint Louis, MO: Parker & Huyett, 1859.

War Department, Report of the Secretary of War, Communicating, In compliance with a resolution of the Senate of February 4, 1867, a copy of the evidence taken at Denver and Fort Lyon, Colorado Territory, by a military commission, ordered to inquire into the Sand Creek massacre, November, 1864.

Whitlock, Flint. *Distant Bugles, Distant Drums, The Union Response to the Confederate Invasion of New Mexico.* Louisville, CO: University, 2006.

Wynkoop, Edward W., edited with an introduction biography by Christopher B. Gerboth. *The Tall Chief, The Autobiography of Edward W. Wynkoop, 1856-1866.* Monograph 9 1993, Denver, CO: Colorado Historical Society, 1994.

Exact Rush

Discover More with Exact Rush

If you found value in Nancy Niero's *Witness at Sand Creek*, we invite you to explore other books by Exact Rush.

Explore Our Catalog

At Exact Rush, we are building a rich selection of titles that focus on culture, spirituality, and identity. From insightful, cerebral non-fiction, to imaginative works that transports you to different realms or teach you something new, our catalog of accurate, informative, and life-affirming titles continues to grow.

Connect with Our Community

Join our community of readers and authors! Participate in engaging discussions, future author meet-and-greets, and exclusive book events. Stay updated by following us on social media and subscribing to our newsletter.

Have a Book Idea?

Do you have a story to tell or knowledge to share? Exact Rush is always on the lookout for unique voices and compelling content. If you have a book idea that aligns with our ethos, we would love to hear from you. Our team is dedicated to nurturing and promoting new talent.

Contact Us

To explore our catalog, discuss a book idea, or to learn more about our services, scan the code here, visit exactrush.com or contact us at: exactrushllc@gmail.com.

www.ingramcontent.com/pod-product-compliance
Lightning Source LLC
Chambersburg PA
CBHW020354170426
43200CB00005B/165